ON
BEING
FROM
NOWHERE

The diary of an
adventure from
Italy to China

ON BEING FROM NOWHERE

The diary of an adventure from Italy to China

Giulio De Osis

JB

First published in the UK in November 2023
Journey Books, an imprint of Bradt Guides Ltd
31a High Street, Chesham, Buckinghamshire, HP5 1BW, England
www.bradtguides.com
Text copyright © 2023 Giulio De Osis
Edited by Samantha Cook
Cover illustration/cover design by Neil Gower
Layout and typesetting by Ian Spick
Map by David McCutcheon FBCart.S
Production managed by Sue Cooper, Bradt & Jellyfish Print Solutions

ISBN: 9781784779801

British Library Cataloguing in Publication Data
A catalogue record for this book is available from the British Library
Digital conversion by www.dataworks.co.in
Production managed by Jellyfish Print Solutions, printed in the UK

To find out more about our Journey Books imprint,
visit www.bradtguides.com/journeybooks

To my parents

ABOUT THE AUTHOR

Giulio De Osis is a pseudonym. The author is an economist by training who in 2017 decided to take a brief detour from his career to satisfy his childhood dream of becoming an explorer. After all, economists and explorers were bound to have more in common than that initial letter 'e'. He has since returned to working as an economist in London. This is his travel writing debut.

TABLE OF CONTENTS

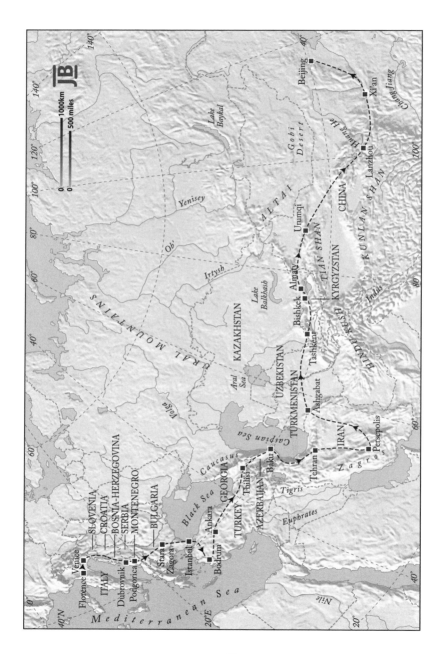

PREFACE

There are many ways this story could be told. Like there were many reasons for this story. Each one incomplete, each one a part. The most truthful reason was that I wanted to travel. But to other people that was not good enough. So I made up more reasons.

I graduated from university in the summer but had no intention of starting work that September. Kaspar, a friend since always, had just finished his third year in the City and was already in need of a break. He resigned from his job, I deferred the one waiting for me and together we decided to set off on the road a few months later.

That would be the short version of how it all started. The longer one involves lots of toing and froing between embassies to obtain visas, countless trips to car mechanics to fix an old Land Rover, and endless daydreams – the latter arguably taking most of our time and resources.

Kaspar was only a year my senior but we were already at very different stages of our lives. He was bordering on burnout, much less optimistic about the many years of work ahead and in desperate need of some time off the runway. An adventure on the road sounded like good medicine: with a departure date, an end date, and just enough exotic charm to justify a brief detour from real life. I, on the other hand, fresh from university, had just finished one of those short life cycles at the end of which one feels like the most senior component of a structure. Head of everything, excited to face anything and mostly unaware that the cycle was about to start anew.

Kaspar and I grew up together in our early years; his home only a few metres from my school and a favoured afternoon playground. We then spent most of our adolescence in distant cities. Our friendship hibernated, only to awaken again as we reached the age to travel independently. At first towards our respective homes, later in places halfway between us and eventually in more distant destinations.

As our travels were rare, we established a ritual for the long intervals of time in between: exchanging a book about someone else's travels. Kaspar's first gift to me was a copy of Paul Theroux's *Dark Star Safari*, a thick tome on the author's overland journey from Cairo to Cape Town. Over the years, that shared library would come to include some of my favourite books, from Nicolas Bouvier's *The Way of the World*, on his years-long drive from Geneva to Kabul, to Rory Stewart's *The Places in Between*, on his walk from one end of Afghanistan to the other.

My first gift to Kaspar was arguably the driest of these reads. For reasons unknown to me today, I handed him a copy of *Il Milione* – the travel accounts of the 13th-century merchant Marco Polo on his way to China. Or at least the alleged account of those travels, given that to some historians it is not clear whether Polo ever made it to China at all.

Either way, that book somehow stuck with us. And over time we discovered that we were not alone: on bike, on foot or by car, many others had set off for the east of Europe with Polo's story on their mind. In his book *In Xanadu: A Quest*, William Dalrymple tells the story of how he retraced Polo's route straight after graduating from university. Freya Stark's 1930s book on her adventures in modern Iran takes its title – *The Valley of the Assassins* – from a story Polo tells. Robert Byron's *The Road to Oxiana*, written in the same period as Stark's book and in the same region, is sprinkled with references to Polo.

We had read about many ways to draw a line on a map, yet, like those other authors, we decided to retrace Polo's – or at least a rough semblance of it. It was not the book per se we liked; but the motion it had powered, the imaginary it had created. It made us feel part of a peculiar community of travellers.

Our starting point was to be Venice and the end Beijing. We even had a standard word to describe our route: the Silk Roads. A term born many years after Polo, but one often associated with him. A noun that in its plural form is sufficiently vague to describe any route starting or ending somewhere between Europe and China. All that gave us more than enough material for a dinner party conversation.

A few months before our departure date I received a call from Anran. I had met Anran sporadically while studying, mostly during lunch breaks outside the university's library. We bonded over our dream of travelling east, which he had done regularly for the past few summers – most recently working as a translator on the Trans-Siberian Express.

When he called me, he was only a few months into his first office job, after having graduated in Russian and Chinese. Like me, he wanted to postpone his career at a desk and spend some time on the road. He had heard about the trip from a mutual friend and had prepared a short pitch on why we should let him join; he told us that he spoke the right languages and would help us find sponsors to cover our costs. I was sold on making space for him in the tent. Kaspar, who had never met Anran, trusted my choice.

Anran eventually made good on his promise to find sponsors. He did so by coming up with another reason for the journey – once again, with the help of a book. The historian Peter Frankopan had recently published *The Silk Roads: A New History of the World*, which notwithstanding (or maybe because of) its grand title had somehow turned into an airport bestseller. Frankopan's view was that history could be retold from a less Western-centric perspective and that the Silk Roads offered the lens to do so. Persia and Central Asia had been an important corridor separating Asia from Europe. When open, this corridor – which itself had had its own major civilisations – had let through art, ideas and often wars, all of which had shaped history in ways that were largely underappreciated.

But what caught our eye was the book's final chapter on the modern Silk Roads. In 2013, China had launched its 'One Belt, One Road' initiative – a one-trillion-dollar infrastructure project and a topic on which Frankopan would later write a follow-up book. The aims of China's initiative were numerous, their priorities unclear. Formally, 'One Belt, One Road' dealt with physical infrastructure and goods – improving the connections between Chinese and European markets, as well as with Africa's and Central Asia's resources. But from an early stage, the project was mired in controversy. Sri Lanka defaulted on Chinese loans for infrastructure projects it could not afford. Greece and Italy sold their largest ports to China, which many saw as a strategic risk. China's rise became tangible and, with it, new fears were being awakened – often from those who saw their influence wane.

This story seemed exciting to us and while we had no experience in journalism whatsoever, a number of construction sites happened to be on our route. We decided to visit these – from highways to train stations – to understand whether China's and the West's media hype around these projects was close to the reality on the ground. A magazine eventually agreed to sponsor us as part of one of their initiatives to support young journalists. A think tank gave us a list of GPS coordinates of sites to visit. Other sponsors followed suit, sending us money or gear.

These were the reasons for our departure – some formal, others less so. After the trip, as I edited my diary, I noticed that none featured much in my notes. Polo appeared only a dozen times, China's 'One Belt, One Road' even less so. The beauty of travel for travel's sake was only exalted in the first weeks, mostly to recount the exhilarating feeling of smoothly crossing borders in Europe. After that, the parables on travel ended.

As Bouvier wisely put it: 'Travelling outgrows its motives'. The reasons for leaving differed entirely from those that drew me to edit my diary as soon as I returned, almost four months later. The main one then being a desire to tell the stories of the people we had met – 'we' being Kaspar, Anran and I: the main subject pronoun in my notes.

'Tell the world about us' is a phrase we often heard at the end of our encounters. It was a strange plea. One that at times revealed the simple aspiration to appear on someone else's map. At others, it seemed to want to repair the tarnished reputation of the pleader's country. As if an interaction could alter our general view of a place. A view that more often than not on our route was inextricably tied up with the autocrats at the helm. Iran was the land of the ayatollahs. Azerbaijan and many of the so-called stans were often associated with their Soviet-era dynasties. These rulers, their ways and a collection of few other stereotypes were all we had in our imaginations.

Travelling changed that. These countries, these places, we now associated with encounters, collections of people and their stories – more complex and more lasting than their leaders. Maybe the pleaders were right. 'Tell the world about us'; I thought I owed some people a try.

I. ITALY

Day 1 – Florence to Venice

What follows is a diary, one I wrote on the road and edited in the years after my return. The order of days provides a flimsy structure to my thoughts, but one I embraced for its meaning. For little did I know, but on this first day I was about to start a time with a timeline – when every day is remembered, defined. A period that stands in contrast to times without timelines, when days and weeks blur into one.

Our symbolic start point was to be Venice but our actual point of departure ended up being my grandparents' garden in Florence. We found a charitable mechanic nearby who was willing to get the car in order for not a lot of money and my grandma agreed to cook a lunch to celebrate our departure. It gave her great pleasure to make sure we were leaving well fed and with an inordinate amount of food supplies on board.

We parked the car on the frosty grass and made an inventory by setting out all our belongings on the ground. It was a crisp February day and the anxiety in my family was palpable. My mum kept circling around taking pictures while my dad asked why we were leaving with so much stuff. What made me anxious was the fact that I knew I now had to make it to China – anything less would be seen as a failure. I had talked about this trip for too long. And yet, many times we had been close to not leaving at all. Kaspar had rung me up after my graduation asking to postpone the departure by a few months, which we did, at the cost of yet more embassy visits to adjust our visas. A week before leaving, the mechanic had told me the car's alarm kept immobilising the motor without apparent reason.

We left after lunch, descending a hill on the edge of Florence, headed towards the highway. The car felt like an overloaded boat, rolling at each turn, shaving the walls along the narrow alleys. We left in silence, incredulous, as if listening for something to go wrong.

It fell to Kaspar's granddad Michael to distract us. He had flown in the previous day to join us for the first leg to Venice. There, we were due to meet Kaspar's parents for a final send-off. Michael was a retired diplomat in his eighties. He lived in West Devon, where he spent most of his time painting in a barn by his house. He was frail, with trembling hands and a thin figure revealed by a cardigan a few sizes too big. As I drove, though, looking towards the road, I noticed that if I had listened to him speak without turning it would have been difficult to tell his age – at least not quickly. For he spoke in tune with us, sharing our same views. Only the colour he unfailingly added to each topic revealed his maturity and extensive experience.

Our favourite topic was the recent Brexit referendum. Almost a year had passed since the British had voted to leave the European Union. And as the referendum result had not set out the form this departure should take – but only its necessity – the opposing camps had moved further apart since. Kaspar, Anran and I had supported the camp to remain in the European Union, and now that a choice had been made, wanted to salvage a 'softer' exit. But as time passed, the political discourse had become extreme rather than conciliatory, loud not contemplative. Soon enough, Theresa May – the British prime minister at the time – would find the platform to state that 'if you believe you are a citizen of the world, you are a citizen of nowhere'. It was an attack on our way of being, on what we hoped to be. And knowingly or not, we too had become angry.

Michael's take was different; he was disappointed – a state that allowed for more introspection. He had worked his whole life for the European Union and now felt like a schoolteacher whose students have failed. Borders were thickening again, just as we were getting ready to cross them. Nationalism was on the rise not only in Britain – Donald Trump had been elected in the United States a few months prior and Marine Le Pen was soaring in the French polls. But the main thing Michael wanted us to think about was how lucky we were to be able to go. To have the right passport and enough money. It was a luxury we should not take for granted but cherish. For a start, that would quell our anger.

Day 2 – Venice

In Venice, Carnival had just passed and only seagulls were still out to feast. We spent the day pilgrimaging to the square where Marco Polo's house had once been and a few other sites. The three of us could have been mistaken for a sports team – full of energy and all dressed in the same clothes that our sponsors had sent us.

At night, we sat around a bottle of whiskey while Michael told us stories. Brexit and the rise of populism remained favourite topics. As it got late, Michael held up his briefcase, took out three thick letters and handed them to us. Each one had the following phrase written on the front: 'To be opened only in case of emergency, punctured tyre or extreme boredom'. Inside I could feel something the size of a book but with softer edges.

Day 3 – Venice to Trieste

In the morning, we said our goodbyes to Kaspar's family and picked the car up in a parking lot on the mainland. We were headed to Trieste, and from there to the Balkans.

As we circled around the gulf that separates the Adriatic's two major cities, we stopped to visit the remains of Venice's ancient predecessor: Aquileia. The Romans had built this border outpost from the 2nd century BC onwards, and it eventually grew to become one of the empire's largest cities. But of that past much had to be imagined. A few mounds, broken marbles and the vague floorplans of fallen palaces survived. Above the overgrown weeds, only a long colonnade stood proudly. The Hun invasion, six centuries after the city's birth, razed Aquileia to the ground. Those who fled in time did so towards the lagoon nearby – a safer, more isolated place. The same lagoon that would eventually become Venice.

Once near Trieste, we parked our car in a campsite on a hill overlooking the sea. This was the only place we had booked for the upcoming months. From then on, we had no clear itinerary or dates beyond those set in our visas.

To set the tone on our first camping night we took great care to divide tasks with diplomacy: one cooked the pasta; one checked the car; and one unfolded the tent on the rooftop. The tent, which had a tarp made from foil, was accessed by clambering up the front of the car to reach a small ladder that spanned the height of the windshield. The car would clamour at each of our steps as we climbed on to its hood and, from there, via the ladder into the tent. Inside, we had enough space to fit a single thin mattress and three sleeping bags, alternating heads to toes.

II. THE BALKANS

Day 4 – Trieste to Poreč

We left Trieste to head south, along the Adriatic coast of the Balkans – until our fortunes decided against that, turning a laid-back departure into our worst nightmare. As I drove along a tree-lined avenue, I was met by a car coming from the opposite direction. The avenue was tight and I decided to move on to a sidewalk to let the car through. The boot was overloaded, blocking my rear view, so I opened my door to look back as I reversed. I then gathered enough speed to climb on to the sidewalk and suddenly I heard a crash.

For a few seconds no one could figure out what I had driven into. I then looked towards my left and saw that the door I had opened was stuck in the bark of a tree. I moved the car forward to assess the damage. The door had changed shape; folding slightly inwards in a V-shape. At first, thinking this was mostly an aesthetic problem, I was relieved. I then slammed the door to close it, but it bounced back. I slammed it again – this time even harder – only to hear an awful metallic sound. The door no longer fit in the frame; a simple but tragic problem.

Kaspar and Anran went in search of a quick fix. I hoped they could find one before their anger found me. They pulled out our brand-new toolbox and looked at each tool, but none seemed of use. We then agreed to find a mechanic, setting off with an open door. Only a few streets away, we found one on the ground floor of a residential building. A bald, friendly man in a red overall listened to our story: the full one, including the bit about our destination being China. I wondered what he must have thought of that ambition, for he did not show either pity or excitement. Instead, he pulled out a hammer and started slamming it against the door, flattening it with each hit. A crude approach, which after a few hits left us with a scratched but flat door.

Once he was done, he did not ask for money. Instead, he asked to put a sticker of his shop on our car and took a picture of it. He told us we had a long journey ahead, and that he was happy to be part of it in some way. Four days in and we had already relied on the kindness of a stranger. It also turned out to be the first bonding moment between Kaspar and Anran. From then on, they would often find ways to make fun of my driving skills.

We finally left Trieste and entered the Istrian peninsula, passing its towns – packed on thin strips of land extending into the sea like arrowheads. At dusk, we left the highway near the town of Poreč, following a path into a thicket. We set up camp in a clearing, hidden from the mainland but overlooking the sea. It had rained heavily that afternoon and the air was humid. Kaspar somehow lit a fire and we sat around it, observing the red lights of fishing boats passing in the moonlit bay. We remained watchful until late, fearful a police boat could see us and fine us for wild camping. But we were just beginners; it was early March and no one would come searching along that empty coast.

Day 5 – Poreč to Plitvice

Our itinerary for the Balkans was a long wish list pieced together by reading online guides on the top ten things to do in the region. A zigzag between the mainland and coast, which we soon straightened in favour of a smoother route – one drawn to fit our anxiety to move east, where the border with our imagined Orient was. The Balkan landscape was still too familiar and we could drive through Slovenia and into Croatia as if changing regions of the same country. The Orient as we imagined it would stick out suddenly, a jack-in-the-box toy with a border as its crank.

Talking to my family on the phone, though, I came to realise they did not see the transition into the Balkans being as smooth as we did. A view they summed up with a short warning at the end of my calls: 'Be careful in the Balkans.' What I had to be careful of they could not tell me. Even so, their statement bothered me, more so for its paternalism than for its prejudice.

Only later I would understand. The Balkans had been synonymous with conflict for my parents' generation, and with a violent exodus from Istria for my grandparents' one. For decades, a wall cut in half the streets and squares of the Italian town of Gorizia and the adjacent Slovenian settlement of Nova Gorica. When the wall finally fell in 2004, I was too young to remember, and even more so to understand. 'Be careful in the Balkans' was their jumbled-up way of exorcising those memories.

We drove on along the coast, stopping in Poreč and Rovinj to see the cathedrals. Arriving in winter at these seaside towns felt like spying on a party that was not yet ready. The places we passed were guarded, not maintained, with empty parking lots and bathroom floors covered in pine needles. The alleys' wet cobblestones glared under the sky's grey light, as bursts of rain came and went from the sea.

We then headed to Plitvice: a national park famed for its terraced lakes, tied together by streams and waterfalls. The park was in the region that had once been the Republic of Serbian Krajina, a self-proclaimed state that declared its independence from Croatia during the Balkan wars. The Republic only lasted about four years; in 1995 the region was reannexed into Croatia. But the violent turmoil of those years was still apparent. Since we had turned inland, the landscape had lost its glare but kept its desolation. Towns rich in white marble felt like distant memories in this land of alpine forests, abandoned factories and half-built houses.

Before dark, we found a place near the park's entrance named Camp Bear – a large wooden building with a statue of a bear by its side. The room was cheap, but Anran insisted on negotiating further with the owner. His view – on which we would come to disagree – was that when travelling one should always see prices with a foreigner's eyes. To understand the local value of something, one had to converse. Negotiation was a process of discovery; one he took for granted in almost every context.

He turned out to be right about this one, for the room was grimy and small, made of makeshift boards held together with a thin paint of cement. The lights kept cutting off as a storm started to thunder outside. Tired and wet, that night we each had a pain of our own. Only a few days in, life on the road had already started to take its toll.

Day 6 – Plitvice to Pakoštane

We spent the morning wandering around the park with a group of Korean tourists. A path on wooden stilts edged above the moving water, playfully criss-crossing along the insides of a canyon. The lakes turned from grey to emerald to azure and back, in a dance led by the clouds above.

We then drove back to the coast to set up camp. Anran had some friends who had stopped in a seaside town called Pakoštane and they knew a place nearby where we could camp freely. Once there, we placed the car facing the sea, opened the tent and put our chairs on the beach. We sat there, listening to the heavy breathing of the waves on the pebbles. All the while, the sky before us cleared for the first time in days.

Day 7 – Pakoštane to Baška Voda

Long chunks of our days were spent in the car, taking turns to snack, read or sleep in the back. Anran most often took care of the music, Kaspar of podcasts – political ones being his favourites. I preferred driving, for the repetitiveness of the roads soothed me.

But the one thing we all returned to was a CD by Dire Straits. We would often sing along. Other times, we'd wait for the guitar to launch into one of its solos. The notes would gather momentum, their tempo rising in a sort of chase, leaving us hoping the song could only just have started, its energy too strong to end. Then suddenly the track would turn to its fade, and tricked we would gasp for more – over and over.

We pushed on south along Croatia's coast, in awe at the rolling sequence of islands and peninsulas. Along the way, we stopped in Trogir and Split – two towns whose walls had harboured a long series of rulers. Romans, Venetians and Austro-Hungarians – each had left their trace. After our visits, we drove closer to the border with Bosnia and found a campsite just before the highway turned inland. The place was shut for the season but it had half-open toilets and a parking lot overlooking the sea.

A French couple had also parked their van there. They were shy but friendly, and soon enough we were touring the interior of their van, which turned out to be their only home. They had painted the outside by hand with an immense doodle of dark blue waves, while inside they had built a minuscule kitchen counter and a bed with wooden drawers. Together with their shepherd dog, they had been touring the Balkans for a year and were now making a slow return to France to earn some money. We decided to have dinner together, placing their portable grill between our respective homes.

But within minutes, our conversations were cut short. Heavy rain hit suddenly and the couple took cover in their van while we ran to the nearby bathrooms. There we ate wet loaves of bread while a family of hungry cats – who had taken ownership of the place – became increasingly daring in their approaches.

Day 8 – Baška Voda to Dubrovnik

The wind grew so strong in the night that it unlatched the flysheet of our tent. We rushed out, scrambling in the rain to release it from the branch of a tree that had caught it. Once back in the car, we shared a pack of cookies in silence and left for Bosnia.

We arrived in Mostar just after sunrise, planning to spend the day wandering on foot before returning to Croatia at dusk. The contrast with the seascapes we had just left behind was stark; the views closed by mountains and lush valleys, the roads in a poor state. The city centre was partly renovated and partly derelict, skeletons of old buildings riddled with bullet pockmarks. Their presence was so central in Mostar, it seemed that intent rather than negligence had left them there.

We were drawn to Mostar by the Stari Most Bridge: a limestone ribbon closing the deep cut of the Neretva River. Two towers on each end guarded the wide, arched structure, an arch whose steepness favoured elegance – for distant viewers to admire – over the comfort of those walking across. Around the bridge, stone buildings and cobbled streets had been neatly renovated, forming a historic centre for tourists and hagglers to convene.

Kaspar and I walked through with a quick pace, both tired by the constant interactions. Anran – who cherished these – engaged with those who engaged with him, without buying memorabilia nor inducing offence, and somehow leaving all those involved with a smile. The many hints of the city's violent past had left him thirsty for answers, and he seemed determined to get these from someone other than ourselves.

We eventually came across a haggler who offered to take us to his cousin's restaurant. Kaspar and I were both sceptical, but Anran was dead set on following him. With a smirk on his face, Anran looked at us and referred to the man as 'our fixer' – a nod to the protagonist of *The Fixer*, Joe Sacco's comic book on the Balkan Wars. We gave Anran a chance, for on a second look the man was far less threatening than the murky protagonist drawn by Sacco. His defining features were a deep set of wrinkles, a beret and a lumberjack ensemble that gave him an almost studied air of dependability.

We followed the man to a restaurant on the outskirts of Mostar. The place was empty and the lights were off, but we were offered a large plate of lasagne for a reasonable price, so we took it. Once seated around a table, we got to Anran's real motive for this lunch outing: his desire to ask questions. At first, the man spoke little, and even less so about himself. He only warmed to us upon hearing I was Italian; he had found work in a factory in northern Italy at the start of the Balkan Wars and still felt a close connection to his town there.

When we finally asked him about the war, he told us Mostar had been a cosmopolitan city but that the war had changed that. Sniper fire from the mountains enforced a regime of fear on anyone below, and people had recoiled in their neighbourhoods. The famous bridge we had walked across, connecting the east and the west, was destroyed by Croat bombs – only to be reconstructed after the war. Ever since, the city had remained divided into a Croat West Bank and a Bosnian East Bank, a Catholic West and a Muslim East. All this he explained in a matter-of-fact way.

The man's story reminded me of something the Italian journalist Paolo Rumiz had written in his memoir of the war, *Maschere per un massacro* ('Masks for a massacre'). Rumiz explained his struggle to distinguish the many fronts of the war. Some journalists blamed the conflict on the region's ethnic divisions, others on its religious ones. Others still, saw it as a war of the impoverished countryside against the cosmopolitan elite in cities like Mostar and Sarajevo – an opportunity for the former to raid the riches of the latter. Rumiz came to believe that there never was one clear line between the fronts until, at the end of the war, there was.

When we asked the man for his view on all this, he ignored the question on the count of his poor English. When pressed further, he veered into a strange world of conspiracy theories, in which powerful foreign families and external powers had decided the fate of the war. Soon enough, tired by his own story, he paused and said, 'Do not try to make sense of things in the Balkans, it will drive you crazy.' He wanted to talk about football and Italian songwriters, and so we did.

We drove back to the border through a landscape of bare hills and pleasant turns. Around us, the sky's dark hue dripped on to the earth below, covering it slowly in its embrace.

Once over the border and near Dubrovnik, we stopped in the parking lot of an abandoned campsite and again found some fellow travellers who had had the same idea. This time their home was a Toyota with a compact trailer on the back – modern and well kitted out.

Curious to make their acquaintance we knocked on the trailer's door. A dog responded with a flustered bark, a few whispers followed – seemingly trying to quiet the dog. But the barks grew louder and, after a long moment, a face appeared from a fogged window. Finally, the trailer door opened and a puppy ran towards us.

A man and a woman appeared next, both with a broad smile – one that made it impossible to tell what we had just interrupted. Their names were Pia and Martin and, together with their dog Emma, they were driving back home to Germany after a sabbatical spent circling from Scandinavia to Siberia, and back round through Mongolia, the stans, Iran, Turkey and now the Balkans.

They had married before leaving but their hands still searched for holds on the other's body. Martin had a typically Nordic look: he was tall, had a full red beard and playful blue eyes. Pia was of a far darker complexion, with a mane of curly brown hair. And while she was more talkative than Martin, her presence was serious.

I envied their courage to travel together, their acquired traits of accomplished explorers, their calm. Both were generous in dispensing their stories, even when we made it clear we would mostly listen. As they spoke, one could sense the rough, frenzied form a memory takes when it is told for the first time. In no particular order, they talked of the Russian tanks they had met in northern Georgia, of a night spent watching videos of Australian surfers in bikinis while staying as guests of a young man in Tehran; we all laughed at their story of a mouse that decided to spend a week hiding in their car, driving them and Emma insane.

They gave us advice too, largely on how to handle borders and police checks – both of which had been taxing en route. In their view, camp chairs were an invaluable tool. When asked for money on made-up charges, they had learned to set out their chairs by the side of the road and sit patiently with a book. Waiting for the police to tire of their sit-in was, they thought, the safest and most peaceful way not to pay bribes.

In between these stories, an intermission occurred. While Pia and Martin talked, we prepared dinner with our gas cooker. Suddenly, the tip of the gas tank caught fire – not the metal hob, but the tank itself. A tall flame rose on all sides of our cooking pan and Kaspar instinctively capsized the table on which the cooker stood, kicking the gas tank to one end of the parking lot. The tank swirled on itself as Pia caught Emma's collar and Martin did a run for the fire extinguisher in his car. Within instants, a murmur was heard and the fire died out. We all took our misfortune comically and made up for it by eating cheese my grandma had packed neatly for us in Florence.

Day 9 – Dubrovnik to Budva

From Dubrovnik, we covered the short leap to the border with Montenegro and continued south, circling around the Bay of Kotor. The bay combines the imposing traits of a Nordic fjord with the welcoming features of the Mediterranean coast. Rugged mountains drop steeply into the sea, leaving a thin patch of land for well-proportioned towns to nestle on.

Once we were clear of the bay's views, the aftertaste of that beauty was cleared violently by the sight of Budva – an urban sprawl of hastily built cement towers, encircling a long beach. The place is so characteristic of poor urban planning that the term 'Budvanisation' has apparently entered in use in the region to define just that. We stopped nonetheless; tired and in urgent need of a shower, we found a room and headed for a beer on the empty seafront.

Day 10 – Budva to Lake Skadar

South of Budva, the cement ends and an evergreen bush of pine trees carpets the view – preserved by a luxury resort on the nearby islet of Sveti Stefan. Spring had not yet started but seemed suddenly in sight; the day was just warm enough to make the sea enticing, so we parked the car and walked along the beaches, exalted by our solitude and the approach of that midway season. In the scrubs nearby, the cicadas sang and the resin gave its sweet, ancient smell.

We then turned ninety degrees, finally due east. The road rises into the mountains, towards Lake Skadar – a park split between Montenegro and Albania. The lake takes the shape of an immense open arena on which slim wooden canoes criss-cross shyly. Mountains form the stands; and we, as awestuck spectators, followed a tight road perched on these. We drove north, to where the lake narrows into loops of horseshoe canyons and, in still water, floating meadows and water lilies come to rest.

The steep cliff made the area mostly inhospitable, yet some locals had set out stands on the side of the road. They sold cheese and honeypots piled on to tall shelves that glared in the sun. We stocked up for the night and carried on, descending to a village at one of the lake's estuaries and then rising again to a hamlet of abandoned new builds. Overlooking the water a few hundred metres below, we picked the house with the best view and set up camp there.

Once it was dark, we sat around the fire, thankful for a windless night. The car radio played in the background as we passed around a knife and a piece of cheese. And that would have been the end of another quiet day.

In our book, though, a knife and a piece of cheese provided more than enough material to cause trouble, as Kaspar found out – slipping the first through the second and into his knee. Stunned, he looked at me and said, 'I've cut myself,' showing me the drop of blood that had started to gather. I did not make much of it, until I saw his face turn white. It was only then that Anran rushed to the car's first aid box while I, at a loss for words, helped Kaspar lie on the grass floor. He looked towards the sky as we covered his cut. Finally, we fed him a spoonful of honey and saw him regain colour.

In my mind, Kaspar had always been the strongest of the three of us. We were all close in height, but physically Anran and I were almost puny by his side. He was also the calmest; more often than not shrugging off fears Anran and I otherwise fed each other. He always had a solution, a way through; and if he thought there was none, he saw no point worrying about it. Even so, despite his laid-back ways he had an Achilles heel. As he would later admit, the sight of blood – especially his own – was enough for him to come undone.

Day 11 – Lake Skadar to Tutin

We reached Podgorica in the morning. Once past the capital's wide avenues we continued inland, towards the Serbian border, arriving only at nightfall under torrential rain.

The border was not much more than a highway toll station with no roadblocks or queues. Lost in thought, and used to EU borders, I drove through without slowing, only to suddenly hear the shouts of people running behind the car, calling for us to stop. I slammed on the brakes and reversed towards where two police officers waited for us with their machine guns at hand. I was asked to step outside and follow them to a hut nearby. There, they left me standing under the rain, while I watched them sit inside, checking our documents slowly, passing them back to me one by one as a form of punishment. One I accepted with zealous grace. Like bouncers, border guards are a class whose power I'd been taught one is better off not questioning.

Day 12 – Tutin to Niš

Again, we drove all day, this time crossing Serbia from west to east. It was hard not to appreciate days like this, when we had nothing but one objective: reaching another town or campsite. A task that could be approached in any state of mind: drowsy for the lack of caffeine, tossing and turning in the back seat, or even with trepidation.

The distance we had to cover was not long per se, but the fog and snow forced us to drive slowly, and at walking speed when the guard rails disappeared from sight. We drove past a ski resort and into a rural landscape, finally reaching Niš at night. The city had been the birthplace of the Roman emperor Constantine the Great. In more recent times, it had turned into a manufacturing hub. We stopped in a neighbourhood of tall residential towers, housing a vast army of workers. On the ground floor of one of these, a room with bunk beds had been set up as a hostel for passers-by. That night, it was just an old Belgian man and us. I wrote two bullets in my diary, both about this man: he guides off-road tours in the Balkans, his snoring is barely human.

Day 13 – Niš to Stara Zagora

We had sped through much of Montenegro and Serbia as I had been keenly waiting to reach Bulgaria. Diego, a family friend, had invited us to stay at his place in Stara Zagora, a city in the middle of the country. He had been one of my dad's classmates in high school and together we had spent many of my childhood summers. Over time, he had turned into all but an adoptive uncle.

Almost seven years had passed since I had last seen him. Enough years for him to get married, have twin boys and move from Milan to Stara Zagora with his Bulgarian wife Krasina. He had no family or job left in Milan, while she had her parents in Stara Zagora, so when the news of the twins arrived they packed up and moved.

When we got off the highway we found them on the kerbside of a busy road, waving a cardboard sign saying 'Silk Road Office Bulgaria'. Little more than the colour of his beard had changed; he still had the same thin figure, the same joyfulness that always made him the most loved adult on the beach. The one adult who invariably agreed to take his friends' children on a trip to a water park or karting, even in the warmest hours of the day – when parents napped and you were meant to hear a pin drop.

Like a child, he could not keep still. His friends even had a small act they would do to mimic his ways with affection. They would walk back and forth muttering meaningless words, typically 'ken, ken, ken'; sounds not too far removed from those made by murmuring chickens. Once every four years, though, something clicked and then yes, then he would stop. It was the summer Olympics that did it. When the season came, he would find ways to build a small TV set by the pool; and from the opening ceremony to the closing one he would not move, too afraid to miss even the most obscure race.

He had devoted that same intense energy to planning our stay. Stara Zagora did not stand out for its beauty and within an afternoon we had walked through its main sites. But we were the first visitors he had had since moving and Krasina, his two children and a handful of others were his only contacts with the outside world. He could not yet speak a word of Bulgarian and he almost never went back to Milan due to a crippling fear of flying. We could stay for as long as we wanted; his to-do list somehow covered a full week of activities – clashing with our plan to stop for no more than two nights.

That first evening he gave us a tour of some apartments he was refurbishing. He made a small adventure out of it and, enthralled, we followed him. Diego was a master of reinvention; he had studied medicine, had worked in advertising for most of his life and had now decided his passion was interior design. In Stara Zagora, he bought new builds, furnished them with his 'Italian taste' and resold them at a profit. He even had two sets of business cards: one set had the title 'Inferior Designer' printed on them. Business was not booming but his few clients seemed to love the humour.

Day 14 – Stara Zagora

By breakfast we had already agreed to stop a few days longer than planned. We woke up late, the bread on the table was warm and the coffee was good. Most of all, we could spend the morning staring blankly at the television, allowing Kaspar and Anran to catch up with the latest happenings in football.

The two had started to bond, and it was not just a shared passion for football that showed it. The courteousness of the first few days was gone. Instead, they both felt enough affinity to let a new dynamic set in: taking turns to form groups of two and gang up on the third, mostly amicably. Each pairing had its own points of attack. I was an easy target for my tendency to over-plan and over-stress about pretty much anything: the car, the itinerary, supplies. Kaspar and I played on Anran's stinginess or his need for validation when taking even the smallest decisions. Kaspar, on the other hand, was far harder to corner in these contests of low-stakes banter. He knew to take things as they came; and that made him inconspicuous, with few sharp edges for Anran and me to work with.

In the afternoon Krasina guided us on a tour while Diego stayed home with the twins. We drove past Kazanlak, an area famed for its production of rose oil and weapons, and soon after reached Buzludzha, our destination. Buzludzha is a difficult place to describe without it sounding like a figment of my imagination. One could say it is an immense cement structure planted atop a mountain in the middle of nowhere; a structure made to look much like a flying saucer from a *Star Wars* film, with a tall tower on one side. Its size was breathtaking.

The site was built during the Soviet era to commemorate a series of events that had taken place on the mountain, including a secret meeting that led to the formation of the Bulgarian Communist Party in the late 20th century. For about a decade the structure was used as the party's headquarters, only to be abandoned after the fall of the Soviet Union.

We circled the building on foot, fighting our way against the mountain's strong winds. Graffiti covered any wall a hand could reach, concrete blocks carved with Soviet inscriptions had been looted and roof tiles had fallen off, leaving the central amphitheatre half-open to the sky. The atmosphere was eerie, intimidating; my imagination half-expected a stormtrooper to appear from behind any corner.

Once back in the car, Krasina explained that there had been some proposals to repair the site and for it to host a museum of Bulgaria's Soviet history. The money to do so, though, was hard to come by and she joked that it was probably better that way. What better museum of Soviet history than the existing one: a monument containing its birth, utopian vision, hubris and death.

Day 15 – Stara Zagora

We got bogged down in comfort, Diego's huge choice of gins and Krasina's attentions. Only a strict agenda got us off the sofa: to visit a local brewery where a guide showed us around, visibly bored. Straight after, we rushed back to the sofa, occasionally peeking at the parking lot below, making sure our car was still in sight.

Day 16 – Stara Zagora

For our last day Diego prepared the most unusual plan. On a weekend morning we were escorted through his apartment's landing to his neighbour's door. The neighbour Yordan was a larger-than-life character who – Diego thought – we had to hang out with.

When the door opened, we were welcomed by a bulky man in his late thirties, wearing flip-flops and a bathing suit on a cold mid-March day. Yordan spoke some English on account of his international car business. He described his job as bringing European cars to wherever laws made it tricky to do so. At one point he jumbled the words 'container', 'Mercedes' and 'North Korea' in a sentence while we followed him through the apartment. But he hated serious talk and would not let us probe further. If we were his guests, it was not to talk about work but to play with his toys. The house was full of these; there were shiny motorbikes in the garage, marble-plated television sets and a kitsch collection of samurai swords. The toy he prided himself on the most was an AK-47 rifle which he kept unloaded on a sofa (I mistakenly sent a selfie I took with it to my parents, setting off a long number of panicked calls that evening).

He took a strong liking to us. He was a big boy – with a wife and daughter – but still a boy, visibly excited to have three friends over to play with. He renamed Anran, who was British but had Indian origins, as Sanjeev: the main character of a Bollywood film he had recently watched. He was boisterous and oftentimes racist, with a particular dislike for Roma people, 'Gypsies' in his words, blaming them for pretty much any problem he could think of.

After about an hour, he got so excited that he convinced Diego to allow him to take their respective families and us on an afternoon drive to the nearby city of Plovdiv – which we did – all fitting in his minivan. We stopped to see the city's Roman amphitheatre, its Ottoman town houses and its hip streets, far wealthier than those of Stara Zagora.

Yordan even bought us fortune bracelets from an old lady. He wanted us to stay for a few more days so we could have more adventures together; we had to go to a shooting range, and there was a big 'Russian-themed party' we could not miss.

III. TURKEY

Day 17 – Stara Zagora to Istanbul

Instead, we readied to leave, and did so with a pinch of pride. The pride of those who enjoy something intensely and still manage to let go. But really there was little pride to be had; we had stayed as long as we could. The next day my dad was flying into Istanbul to spend a week with us and we had to meet him there.

Diego, Krasina and the kids gathered around the car to wave us goodbye. Yordan dropped by to hand us a large pack of Red Bull cans as a parting gift. We honked and set forth; past the Turkish border, past Edirne and towards Istanbul.

And long before we expected it, Istanbul appeared in front of us. Some forty kilometres away from the Bosphorus we were already in the midst of its tall towers, shopping malls and standstill traffic. Cement in its various forms stretched across hills and hills, long beyond our line of sight. Soon enough, our GPS abandoned us; new roads had been built too recently for its maps to work. We remained trapped in the same few roundabouts until chance brought us in sight of the sea and, along an avenue named after Kennedy, we finally reached the centre.

Day 18 – Istanbul

Our room was in the central neighbourhood of Fatih. We had found it online at a price that seemed too good to be true; a hunch that turned out to be accurate for the place was filthy and had no windows.

We started our day by moving to a hostel for twice the price. All in a horrible mood, we split up saying we wanted to see different things, but really in need of a break from each other.

I headed for the Galata bridge; a bridge whose architecture is largely unremarkable but with a name that had been on my mind. Leonardo da Vinci had drawn a plan for it that was never built. Michelangelo was invited by the then Sultan to do the same, but never did. Today, the bridge connects the modern to the ancient part of the city; a two-storey vein bringing together all forms of people. On the upper level, hundreds of fishermen wait patiently, cigarette in hand. Passers-by rush through, while hawkers sell worms as bait and doughnuts from silver plates they carry on their heads. On the lower level, fish restaurants line up almost at water level, facing the strong smells of the Bosphorus.

In the evening we reunited for dinner in a university district. We were the only Westerners there. Tourism had slowed since a recent terrorist attack and locals seemed happy to see us. Many there were migrants from the east who had come to Istanbul for work. Next to us, two Kurdish taxi drivers enjoyed a narghile. A group of Uzbek youngsters worked as waiters; they understood Turkish and that had made their move easier.

Anran spoke with the Uzbeks in Russian. They were excited to hear we would visit their homeland and between trips to serve tables they would stop to show us pictures of their families. It made us feel awkward. They had moved west, some hoped to go further to Germany. All the while, the European Union had frantically handed Turkey billions of euros to block migrants from heading west via Greece or Bulgaria. Any migrant who travelled irregularly from Turkey would be returned to Turkey, or be stuck in a legal limbo in a refugee camp.

The number of refugees, many travelling from war-torn Syria, had soared over the past few years. Panicked politicians had tightened borders, pushing the problem on to the outskirts of the European Union – no matter the cost, no matter the values at stake. We had the privilege of driving east, of leaving the European Union of our own will. We had crossed the Turkish border the previous day in not more than an hour. For those going the other way, it could take months, not happen at all, or become a matter of life and death.

All that we could not put to words there and then. We could only hear Kaspar's granddad Michael reminding us to be grateful for our two fortunes: the right passport and enough money. Two fortunes we had to learn to treat as just that, fortunes.

My dad arrived that night. He had planned to join us on one of the more historical sections of the trip: our crossing of western Turkey. If it had been us, we would have sped straight east. He insisted we should veer south in a slow drive from Troy to Bodrum, the home of Herodotus in the southwest. Along the way, my dad wanted us to stop in every ancient Greek and Roman city he could find. The point of having an Ithaka, a destination to reach, he would say, was to have a good reason to travel.

I was happy to have him on board. All three of us could have done with more in-depth knowledge on the history of what surrounded us. While an engineer by training, my dad prided himself on an interminable knowledge of the classics, on which he drew constantly. He was in part a product of Italian high schools, and another part a product of his own interest. I had learned from him to look at the world with range, for the best insights about one's own field were often found in the least expected places. Walking with him through our city of Rome, I would discover new stories in the most common places. Each marble had a faraway home, each deity a family tree and each church a Pope.

When I was growing up, his seriousness had long scared off my classmates. Whenever they'd come over to play, I would get the question 'Are your parents home?', which really meant 'Is your dad home?' I blamed it on the dark eyebrows and his pensive expression. One could have easily taken him for formal. I don't think he could help it but he had built an aura of respectability, one he knew when to shrug off. And when he did so, which he did cautiously, it left those present happy to have been part of it.

Also, as much as I didn't like to admit it, I owed much of my passion for travel to my parents. Travelling together on a journey I had organised felt like a rite of passage. It was also a helping hand on that passage. The road was long, full of pitfalls and opportunities to step back. His decision to join was a way to stand behind my choice, smoothen the ride and give a little nudge to go ahead, because he too thought this was worth something.

My dad had become committed to my project, and had his own fears and fantasies about it too. His main fear was that I knew nothing about cars and that would come back to bite me at some point. A fear followed closely by that of me getting arrested, in all likelihood for voicing my political views in the wrong place or with my youthful hot-headedness.

He would only joke about these fears with me, but months after my return I would learn that he took them more seriously than I thought. On the day I had left, he had taken a vow not to drink a sip of alcohol until my return. Even as an engineer, he knew that luck was the best grease to bring on our journey.

Day 19 – Istanbul

From the moment my dad arrived, we turned into students on a school trip. We noticed how much aimless wandering we had done before. Our rhythms slowed; now we started our days with a long sit at a bar, ordering orange juice and observing passers-by. My dad would open his guidebook and share his plan. We would then follow him trustfully to wherever he'd take us.

Of the places he brought us to one struck me in particular. It was a spot we had passed many times the previous day without even noticing. On an esplanade between Hagia Sophia and the Blue Mosque lies the city's ancient hippodrome and, at its centre, a bronze structure by the name of the Serpent Column. The bodies of three snakes twist on each other, reaching towards the sky. The heads at the top of the column have been cut off, but the tight grip of their bodies makes the column appear like a rope still being pulled from above.

The column was built to commemorate the Greek victory against the Persians in the Battle of Plataea during the 5th century BC, a battle that stopped the Persian invasion of mainland Greece. The intertwined snakes represent the Greek city states that united to fight an outside force. The column is thought to have been forged with the swords of the vanquished Persians.

The East and West met in Istanbul and that was known; this story fed our hunger to dig deeper into that cliché. It was the ways they met, though, more than the fact that they did, that fascinated us. They met in art and they met in violence. Over and over that would be a theme of our road east. Cultures meet until they don't. Istanbul lived on that thin line, opening and closing with the times, filling with art and culture while peace lasted and then, in cycles, emptying itself with the passing of war.

Day 20 – Istanbul

The downside of travelling with my dad was that we became prey for anyone trying to extort money from tourists. The three of us had never attracted much attention with our studenty appearance. Now that we had a real adult with us, we become a constant target for merchants, beggars and unsavoury characters. Chief among these were Istanbul's taxi drivers.

On one occasion we asked a driver to take us to Hagia Sophia. He drove us in the opposite direction, taking us to a gas station miles away that had the same name. A trick that cost us our time, but that was too preposterous to cost us our money.

Day 21 – Istanbul to Assos

How many times had we been on the road for more than three weeks? No family holiday, no trip with friends had seen us change home so often and for so long. Three weeks was our threshold; one set by most employees, by most people. I wondered whether beyond that travel would stop being a novelty and became a routine.

Three weeks in – and with three months to go – our morale had been on a strange roller coaster. We had faced fear when our car broke down back in Italy. But our excitement about things to come had been so great that fear had healed quickly, like a mosquito bite. Instead, a longer-lasting discomfort had taken hold: that of travelling with a tent in winter. Often wet, often tired, we had cocooned along the cold Balkan roads, recovering at Diego's place from an unfamiliar exhaustion. And although we never formally took stock of it, our health had fluctuated too.

Now, after a week-long break from the road, we had regained our restlessness. Under the auspices of a warm sun, we were back on the road, running away from the city. We headed south, past the many war cemeteries of Gallipoli, to take a ferry across the Dardanelles to the port city of Canakkale. We visited the few remains of Troy, fantasising in front of the open plain that leads to the sea below the city walls. And at night we reached the seaside town of Assos, with its handful of houses and pebble beaches. On the hill behind us, the columns of a Greek temple dedicated to Athena overlooked the sea and the island of Lesbos ahead.

Day 22 – Assos to Çandarli

In travel writing, I noticed writers rarely spoke of what they left behind. It was as if they had no families or partners to think of. Communicating with one's home was a sign of weakness, of being overcome by nostalgia. One always had to look forward, to the road.

But I realised how much all that mattered to us. The will to share was ever-present and at set times we would gather by our phones and do just that. We were not part of a generation who wrote letters; we had to admit that to ourselves. Kaspar and Anran both had girlfriends back home and had to maintain their relationships via a screen. They did so in different ways; Anran would often disappear to speak or text discreetly while Kaspar was far less shy when with his phone. We could only update others so often and we knew that soon enough we'd be off the grid for days at a time.

Sharing defined our moods. Guilt for being away for so long took turns with pride and a sense of satisfaction. Calling home supported us; it gave us perspective on what we were doing, reminding us of what we could have been doing instead. And there were fights with the loved ones at home too. These would leave the one of us who was involved pensive, while the other two played their part to soften the inevitable return to the present, the road.

Day 23 – Çandarli to Bodrum

We had not fully grasped the scope of my dad's ambitions. In the space of two days, we had seen one ancient Greek city after another.

We started in Pergamon, with its remains perched on a tall hill, surrounded by rivers below. A city so wealthy that a few kilometres away it had a sanctuary for therapeutic retreats. This was the sanctuary of Asclepius, the Greek god of healing; a complex of underground passageways, wide halls and olive groves. People travelled from afar to stop here, and therapies included spas and the interpretation of dreams. Non-venomous snakes were said to roam freely as Asclepius was often represented with a rod in his hand and a snake wrapped around it. A symbol that remains in the iconography of pharmacies to this day.

We stopped in busy Ephesus, with its red marble library, in Priene and finally in Miletus to visit its theatre. This was a network of cities built by the Greeks, wealthy through commerce, and later taken over by the Romans. Priene and Miletus had once faced the sea, but over time their ports had silted up. Now the sea was no longer even visible in the horizon.

They were places built in harmony with their surroundings. Theatres faced the mountains ahead and roads aligned with nature's features. The locations had been picked to leave one in awe, to be eternally beautiful. Seeing so many cities one after the other I was surprised by how consistent the architecture and sense of style was from one place to the next.

I raised this with my dad while we walked through the streets of Ephesus. He pointed out how the frescoes of a Roman villa nearby were in many ways similar to those I had once seen in the villas of wealthy Roman families in Pompeii. In both places, the frescoes were framed by elegant red lines on a white background. If I was surprised by consistency throughout a region of a few hundred kilometres, I was forgetting that the Greeks and Romans had somehow carried their sense of aesthetics through the Mediterranean and beyond. They had established an immense precinct of beauty, one designed to survive, recognisable, to this day.

Day 24 – Bodrum to Pamukkale

On the southwestern coast of Turkey, we had reached the port of Bodrum – a place of modern wealth. Bodrum was a resort where yachts from Delaware and Odessa parked side by side. Brazilian ambient music lulled passers-by on the decks and Italian luxury brands had set up wooden shacks to sell beachwear.

Our way of travel had changed. While before we would have searched for the nearest hostel or campsite, with my dad we had established a new practice. Upon arriving in a town, we'd leave him to wait at a bar and start our search. Anran would lead the pack, asking for rooms at every hotel reception, negotiating the best price. He would then report to my dad what he had found and my dad would pick the most sensible option. At dinner we would eat fish along the coast.

My dad worried we were a stingy bunch, that we would not enjoy things fully. He had always called me Uncle Scrooge, for my resemblance to the character from Disney's comic book and his frugal ways. And it was true, if it were not for him, we would not be living this way. For my part though I was happy the three of us shared the same expectations. None of us had a real clue as to how much this trip would cost. Our sponsors had given us a budget and we kept a mental note of our daily spending. But the fear of going overboard was always in the back of our minds and keeping a tight ship was our way of feeling better.

Day 25 – Pamukkale to Konya

For good measure, we had stopped to see two more Greek cities. Aphrodisias with its immense stadium and Pamukkale with its thermal springs and natural pools of travertine. After that, we were finally due east, moving inland towards Konya.

Snow-capped mountains in the distance marked the edges of an otherwise barren landscape. We passed freshwater lakes and empty salt pans. The temptation to drive through these white deserts was irresistible. It seemed like I could close my eyes and gather speed without risk. So – against my dad's advice – I drove off the road and into one.

I immediately felt the car lose speed. I accelerated but the tyres slipped to a stall, turning on themselves. It did not take long to realise that underneath a thin layer of salt, the pan was a deep pool of mud; a mud so soft that the tyres became as smooth as clay on a potter's wheel.

We were stuck, but at least we had an engineer on board. After giving me the reprimand I deserved, my dad sent us all to find rocks nearby. He had us create two paths with these for the tyres to gain traction on. And after about an hour we had managed to build something long enough for the car to gather speed, float out of the pan and back on the road.

Still covered in mud, we made it to Konya on time for a Sufi ceremony. Every Saturday, the local Sufis gathered in a conference centre to see the whirling dervishes. We sat in a round auditorium while on stage men of all ages swirled with their hands held just above their shoulders. They wore long white robes, with skirts that opened like flowers as they turned. They kept their heads tilted, each one somehow holding on to a tall felt hat.

The place had the ambience of a club, with neon lights of all sorts and powerful bass sounds. A flute ensemble played a hypnotic tune while a deep voice recited a prayer. Twenty or so men swirled together at first, maintaining a perfect distance between each other. They then formed a circle, taking turns to reach a trance in the middle. The younger men showed the greatest fervour in throwing themselves in a fast spin, sweating, with their eyes open but unfocused. The older men turned gracefully and with a pleased smirk on their face. The odd background soon faded from my mind and I felt captured by the swirling, by the emotions of those on stage.

Konya was one of the last places where Sufis still gathered in these ceremonies. It had maintained this tradition because Rumi – the 13th-century Persian poet and father of Sufism – was buried here under a turquoise dome. Rumi was a mystic, an advocate of the use of music and dance as a form of prayer. Spinning in repetition was a way of abandoning one's ego and desires to focus on God.

Over the years I had seen Rumi's poetry in the most unexpected places: on the walls of hostels or on the coffee tables of agnostic friends. His appeal extended far beyond Islam for his poetry was accessible, it spoke of tolerance and love. His poems preached self-acceptance and improvement at the same time; they had a meditative tone but one free from the heaviness of judgement. It was a message that transcended cultures and religions, and one that could still be heard in a mosque in Konya as much as in a yoga class in the West.

Day 26 – Konya to Avanos

In addition to its Sufi past, Konya had featured in my imagination for another reason. Its railway station was on the last surviving branch of the Taurus Express – a railway line that had once extended through much of the Middle East. Built by the Germans in the 1920s, it allowed travellers to take a train from Egypt, Iraq and Iran to Istanbul. From there, one could connect to the line's famous cousin: the Orient Express to Paris or London.

It was a railway line that must have been a source of endless fantasies in the minds of travellers. A line that stayed open until the start of the Iraq war in 2003. Today, all that remained of the Taurus Express ended only a few hundred kilometres east of Konya, in the town of Adana.

I had always loved to draw lines along the rail tracks or roads that connect one country to the next. I daydreamed about how far I could get, how long it would take me. I would speak to my friends of these plans, laugh at their ridiculousness or debate their challenges. From Turkey, my mind had learned to follow the routes east to Iran and the rest of Asia. I saw the main obstacles as deserts or mountain passes, obstacles my lines could circumvent in one way or another. But the routes south, via Iraq and Syria, were closed by something different; a war zone cut through the one overland link separating Europe from Africa. It was an area I often dreamt of covering, a link I hoped would open again someday.

Konya was also the end of the line for my dad's journey. That morning, we drove him to the airport before planning to head east, towards Cappadocia. I could tell the idea of leaving bothered him. He asked about our next stops, about the road to Georgia. Then he went quiet, thinking about the days of work ahead.

His usual goodbye followed: 'Don't do stupid things.' It was a phrase he had used before, mostly when dropping me off at parties as an adolescent. It worked just as well for a road trip to China. The mutual understanding was that I could do stupid things, as long as I did not make him or my mother worry.

A lot would change again for the three of us. We had to give back our comforts, our frequent restaurant meals. We'd lose a party to our conversations and we'd return to being the less mature bunch we had been before. We'd drive from A to B in more spontaneous ways, but there was a depth to our journey that we would probably never have again.

Along a brand new highway, we reached the town of Göreme in Cappadocia. It was a disconcerting place. The houses carved in the soft rock that made Cappadocia famous were neighboured by American fast-food chains. For some reason we had expected to find a place still ancient. Instead, we arrived to find caravans of rumbling quad bikes.

We left in a rush, following one side road after another until those ended and we had to move on along the dry grass. Tall walls of smoothly curved rock tightened into a delicate embrace, finally closing in at the feet of a mountain. Nearby, a door had been carved into the rock and birds had built their own houses in small holes.

Out of nowhere, a man approached us on foot while we set up camp. He must have been a local Bob Marley, with long black hair and a calm expression. Only a slight flicker in his eyes spoke to his surprise at seeing us up there. He had an impressively strong physique and said he owned that piece of land, marked by no borders.

Then, making it clear he did not want us to feel threatened, he told us he expected nothing from us. Having just learned our three nationalities, he repeated in half-broken English: 'Turkey, Italy, France, India, all *compañeros*,' and invited us for tea in a cave nearby.

Day 27 – Avanos

Heavy rain woke us up in the early hours. We waited in silence until morning, then not knowing what else to do, we drove to the town of Avanos to visit a carpet-making cooperative. Our guidebook said they spun silk from cocoons to make certain high-end carpets; we thought we might see what gave the name to our road.

The cooperative was a large two-storey building, with workshops and storage rooms overlooking an internal courtyard. It was almost industrial in size, but we were the only visitors there. Suat, the manager, welcomed us with open arms. He was a good-looking man in his forties, half-French and half-Turkish, with dark curly hair and a hoop earring in one ear.

Suat took our curiosity to heart, unfolding every carpet he could, knowing that we would not purchase any. He showed us how the price of each carpet depended on the number of knots within it. His mood oscillated wildly; he held on to an open smile for entire minutes, suddenly crashing into a sad, often blank, stare. He was impossible to decipher.

He then took us to a room where in a glass container hundreds of silkworms feasted on mulberry leaves. Twenty or so days into their life, the worms start oozing a silk filament, imprisoning themselves into a cocoon. But before the worm can ever escape and become a moth, the cocoons are thrown into a pot of boiling water. They are then stirred with a ladle, until soft enough for the silk to be delicately pulled from the cocoon and spun into a thread. A few thousand silkworms and hundreds of kilos of mulberry leaves barely produce a kilo of raw silk.

It was this odd procedure that the Chinese had managed to keep all but secret for centuries. At first, this lucent material had been reserved for the emperors of China. Slowly though, silk filaments had escaped West – becoming a coveted good for the Greek and Roman aristocracy. Silk was so valued in these societies that the Far East became known as the land of 'Seres', or silk.

Suat told us all this. He was enthusiastic about our story, our route, and took us to eat in the canteen to hear more of it. He introduced us to each one of the workers there. The looms were staffed mostly by women, many of whom had worked there their entire life. Some spoke a foreign language – French, Italian, Russian, Chinese – ready to cater to tourists from anywhere. Only a few years prior, the cooperative had had more than 200 employees, now there were not more than forty left. Like in Istanbul, tourism had declined after a string of terrorist attacks and a failed military coup the year before.

Before we could leave, Suat asked if we could do him a favour. His son was in high school and wanted to study law in Turkey. Suat though wanted him to leave the country – to go to France or the United Kingdom – anywhere but Turkey. He asked us to convince him.

We picked Anran as a spokesperson and awkwardly passed him Suat's phone. With his usual social agility, Anran started the conversation with Suat's son by talking about football. But Suat was quick to interrupt him with a question: 'My son is worried that as a Muslim he will not be welcomed in the United Kingdom, what do you think?'

He would be welcomed, Anran explained, people from all over the world come to study there. Then he added, 'Although no one will welcome you like your dad welcomed us here.'

I saw Suat's face turn into an impossible mix of sadness and happiness, both at once – that same mix we had tried to interpret all along.

Day 28 – Avanos to Ankara

From Cappadocia we drove north to Ankara. We were due to stop by the capital's embassies to get some final visas for Central Asia. The Land Rover was also in need of a check-up before the long stretches of isolated land ahead.

Once there, we let bureaucracy come second and the car come first. A search online sent us to find a mechanic in an immense industrial complex; a place that was the closest thing to an economist's definition of competition. A hundred or more small mechanics' shops lined up next to each other – street after street – and all specialising in a specific part or make. There were shops that sold only oils, tyres or filters, and a handful that fixed Land Rovers, each tailored to a different budget.

We picked a shop that looked neither too cheap nor too expensive. The owner – greasy from head to toe – had a thick moustache that gave him a reassuring look of experience, even as his eyes glimmered with the excitement of a child. He was a simple character, passionate about Land Rovers and, as he was too quick to reveal, Russian escorts. Only few locals owned Land Rovers, so he spent most of his time working on custom fits for foreign clients. Labour was considered cheap in Turkey and he received cars from all over Europe. We understood all this with sign language and the help of an online translator.

The man knew how to unbuild and rebuild a Land Rover like Lego. But his approach to doing so was far more social than expected. First, he jumped on the front seat and asked me to drive him around the neighbourhood. Then, as he bought new sets of oils and filters, he would change these on the spot with the help of whoever had sold them to him. When done, he would jump back on the car and point us to the next shop. We had someone check the tyre pressure, someone align the tyres with the driving wheel, and someone else still check the electrics.

His final contribution was to take a test drive around a construction site nearby. As I sat in the front seat next to him, I discovered the car could climb hills in ways I had never imagined. The motor groaned in pain as the man turned to me with a smile.

At the end of our ride, I looked towards the back seat to find Kaspar and Anran seemingly in two completely different places. Kaspar looked as overwhelmed as I was – not just by the roller-coaster ride but by the long day of social interactions. Anran instead was visibly energised. He seemed to love this place, and had already learned to speak some words of Turkish beyond goodbye and hello. The mechanics addressed him directly, while Kaspar and I quietly accepted our roles as hangers-on.

We had learned to complement each other. Anran was the master of all transactions and things social. I planned everything, ceaselessly. Kaspar, who hated plans, dealt well with the unexpected. He was the level-headed one who knew how to quiet our fears, simply by making it seem like he had none of his own.

Having established these roles, we took turns to play the leading character. A process that happened naturally, for each day seemed to give a chance to one of us – leaving no one on stage for too long and everyone with a moment to reflect on the road.

Day 29 – Ankara

Beyond mechanics, Ankara was also a place of wide avenues, residential districts and government buildings. A capital, but one less deserving of the name than Istanbul. The more we moved east, away from cosmopolitan Istanbul, the more we thought we could see the imprints of a different Turkey, a more conservative one. It was a side of Turkey around which President Erdoğan had built his appeal during his long rule. He had brought forward a nostalgia about Turkey's Ottoman era, placing himself at the centre of its hoped-for revival. He had also given a greater voice to Islam, moving away from Turkey's secularist roots. And in Ankara all this came through in a number of ways; his grip was far tighter here than in Istanbul – where he had once been mayor.

There were hints in the large number of Turkish flags on display, or in the new mosques that seemed to be under construction at every other corner. There were also less subtle messages, like the fact that the city was plastered with posters of Erdoğan's face, and the word '*Evet*!' – which is Turkish for 'Yes!'. A major referendum was a few weeks away and people were being asked to vote in favour of transforming Turkey from a parliamentary system into an executive presidency. A reform that would hand Erdoğan more power. But the opposition and foreign observers were already claiming the 'Yes!' campaign was fraught with irregularities. In Ankara, at least, posters with a '*Hayir*!' – 'No!' in Turkish – were hard to come by.

Day 30–31 – Ankara to the Georgian border

We left Ankara with the satisfaction of having checked the car, done our laundry, and obtained our visas more smoothly than expected. From here, we travelled for two long days along Turkey's northern coast via Samsun and Trabzon, stopping rarely.

One brief stop though was enough to change our light-hearted mood. At a gas station, Anran was tasked with filling the tank. We then drove away normally, stopping again for lunch a hundred or so kilometres later. Here not only did we realise that Anran had forgotten to close the tank, but also that he had left the lid on the pump. We took a sudden U-turn and rushed back to the gas station – now more than an hour away.

It was a testament to Anran's clumsiness, but one Kaspar and I took with little humour. We stayed in silence most of that day, working off our tension without having to fight. It took the sight of the border with Georgia to lift our spirits as the Turkish words for goodbye, or '*Güle Güle*', bade us farewell with their playful sounds.

IV. GEORGIA

Day 32 – The Georgian border to Batumi

Travel guides had warned us of the dangers of driving in Georgia; we were still unprepared for what we were about to see. Most cars looked like carcasses, moving forward thanks to some form of miracle, and on single-lane roads drivers overtook cars that were themselves overtaking. Randomness was the rule of the day, together with having as many eyes open as possible and not trusting others to have any at all.

Our first thought was to buy local insurance as quickly as possible. We asked passers-by to point us to the nearest banks but it was a Sunday afternoon and none seemed open. After a while we stopped trying altogether; a taxi driver had looked at us gravely and said, 'Insurance? The only insurance here is God.'

The border opened straight into Batumi, a seaside city known for its casinos. Past the neon lights and Ferris wheels, we reached its outskirts in a hilly area thick with greenery and walled gardens. We set up camp here, on the first patch of grass we could find – surrounded by wrought-iron gates and the hungry eyes of dogs behind them.

Our presence set forth a barking concert, bringing out much of the neighbourhood. From the crowd an old man came forward to greet us in Russian, with an accent Anran described as almost incomprehensible to him. He had a broad face heavy with wrinkles and wore a cardigan falling on the sides of his round belly. After a few words, he wandered around the car observantly, occasionally tripping on his evening slippers.

His wife soon joined him, wearing a nightgown; they spoke briefly before she went back in to fetch a jar of pickled beets to gift us. We offered them a bottle of whiskey in exchange, which the old man received happily, taking a swig. Otherwise we just stood there awkwardly, shivering in the cold night, until a light rain started and the old man invited us to his basement.

Down there, the air was even more humid; the place was filthy, with nothing but a wooden table and two benches to furnish it. The table's centrepiece was a plastic tank filled with a dense – orange-coloured – wine. The few dialogues that followed were simple; the old man loved Italy and any clichéd Italian word was enough for him to break into an explosive cheer. A game we repeated more and more frequently the drunker we got. The wife occasionally peeked into the room, never joining.

We understood little about the old man's life other than that he had been in jail for the best part of two decades. He had beaten up what – in his words – was 'the wrong guy'. We struggled to picture any violence coming from him, from this old man so afraid of shattering like glass at every step.

To spice up the conversation, Anran decided to ask what he thought about Russia's President Putin. It was then that, without notice, the old man decided to show us what his physique had lost. For what felt like an eternity, the old man held Anran at gunpoint with his stare; his heavy breath and the fizzle of the neon above us now loud in that airless room. The tension rose to the point that even violence – even coming from an old man – seemed possible. Instead, the old man's wrinkles softened, and he broke into a wild laugh. Pointing at our scared faces, he asked we all raise our glasses to Putin; then he stared at Anran again and told him to never ask such questions.

After that, we spoke about nothing. The old man's whiskey finished, and with that we took the cue to leave, staggering upstairs. He insisted on kissing all three of us on the cheek before letting us out. We then gathered in the tent, realising we had not exchanged names once.

Day 33 – Batumi to Gori

Things got even stranger in the morning. We woke up with a terrible hangover, and the old man's wife came out to say her husband was too sick to get up but that he sent us his regards.

Before setting off, I reeled in a state towards a hedge and as I readied myself to pee, two eyes peeked at me from the other side. A big man appeared, coming towards me while blurting out angry exclamations. Anran rushed between us with the speed of a cavalry unit saving the panicked infantry. A few of his Russian phrases miraculously lightened the man up, and it was not long before we were asked to follow him to his house for breakfast.

This time though it was not a basement but a living room; we even picked up the man's name: David. David with the hands and size of a Goliath. A schoolteacher in his early fifties, with a house teeming with people: kids of his own, grandkids and nephews. All gathered in a bare room where the three of us were sat on one of two sofas.

Everyone stopped what they were doing, piling on the other side to look at what David had brought home. They asked about our families, if we had siblings, about their health. They wanted to know what films we liked, their favourites being mostly Bollywood hits – a taste inherited from Soviet times. Anran held the conversation with his fluent Russian; Kaspar and I ate away at a scone-like pastry, offering little in return. We posed for pictures – our heads still pounding – and all the while more people kept arriving. There were neighbours and family; some came in, looked at us and left. Kids burrowed in their parents' arms, until they got fed up and returned to play. Everyone wore layers and layers of sweaters, and in the cold air the steam of our breaths met without ceremony.

David seemed genuinely happy to have us there. He asked us to stay for the night so that we could talk more. We thanked him politely, but slowly made our way out, goodbye after goodbye.

Once in the car, I saw David approach my window. He looked at me, then at Kaspar who was by my side, and said his first words in English: 'Tell the world about Georgian hospitality, tell the world about us.'

His voice was confident, knowing when to pause for effect. Kaspar promised we would do so, while I nodded, filling my silence with the sound of the car starting up. Kids and adults started to cheer, having come to the street to say their farewells. In my mind, they cheered for those who travel, for those who unapologetically do what they like the most. Driving away – towards Gori, towards the centre of Georgia, eastward – I felt a strong sense of righteousness, I felt elated, proud to be travelling.

That feeling did not last long. As the cheers faded from memory, my pride often turned into doubt. I had read somewhere that travellers are cowards, that travel is postponement. You escape your home, you become unstuck and get a fickle sense of freedom. But by seeing the world, by seeking others' roots, you fail to make your own. Travel for travelling's sake becomes travel for one's own sake.

I thought about all this, about what David had asked us. Maybe travel could be less selfish, and David had hinted at how. We had to be messengers, to talk about David, about our encounters.

Before setting foot in Georgia, the only images I could bring to mind when thinking about this country were the scenes of the 2008 Russian invasion, of tanks rushing through bombed cities. There were also some horror stories of the Georgian mafia which occasionally had surfaced in Italian papers, mostly emphasising this mob's similarity to the Sicilian one. I knew the names of a handful of Georgian dishes. But that was it; war, mafia and food – an embarrassing trinity.

Now I had David too; his hospitality, his wish to be remembered. An encounter was enough to make my view of Georgia more nuanced. Telling that story could maybe do the same for others too. And maybe – through that story – I would start to question my own roots. As if by looking at others I could learn to see myself through their eyes. I held on to these thoughts, thoughts I would often return to along the way.

Day 34 – Gori to Tbilisi

The road has a way of making one oscillate between clarity and confusion. In Gori, we fell with both feet into the latter. The spark was our realisation that the city's main museum not only remembers but honours the life of its famed resident: Joseph Vissarionovich Stalin.

Born into a poor family in 1879, Stalin started his career as a bank robber, getting arrested numerous times along the way. The museum shows a police photograph of Stalin in his early twenties, next to reconstructions of his family home and printouts of his first poems.

The museum then tells the story of a wild youth who found his calling as a leader. A rags-to-riches story, Soviet-style. The riches part is summed up in a collection of busts and pictures of Stalin walking along red carpets. The largest room in the museum is dedicated to the gifts foreign officials donated to him over the years.

One would almost be forgiven for leaving the museum thinking Stalin was a Georgian folk hero. Room after room one awaits to see mentions of gulags, of famines and the millions of deaths that made Stalin one of the bloodiest tyrants in history. But all one finds is a half-hearted display at the end of the tour showing the interrogation techniques used by Soviet officials. Nothing more. After that, a tourist shop sells magnets and T-shirts with Stalin's face.

The museum is an ode to strong-man leadership, to the rule of one. An ode I had not expected to find in a democracy, even less so in a country that that had recently gone to war with autocratic Russia.

History had been repackaged. It was a pattern we had seen elsewhere: Istanbul's Hagia Sophia being one such place. This time, though, we could not pinpoint the intent, which made the museum far stranger. Was the Georgian pride in having bred a superstar so tall it could trump the histories of the millions who had suffered?

Day 35 – Tbilisi

In Tbilisi the cherry trees had just started to blossom. For two nights we stopped in a hostel, sharing a room with the typical cast of characters one finds in such places: lonely travellers keen to mingle and talk – often about conspiracy theories – hikers, doctoral students and the lost soul who was meant to stop for a week but had already been there a month, buying potted plants along the way.

We fell quickly for this city. The ancient and the hip were delicately woven together in a pattern that was intricate enough to make anyone curious, but not so intricate as to be hard to revel in. Bars seemed like houses, and houses like bars, and between the two we could change floors and walk through buildings without knowing clearly which was which. In the old centre, we opened doors to find courtyards with wooden façades and balconies on which we were free to wander, making the pavements creak without the fear of being caught and told off. It was a game we could play endlessly, running through this labyrinth; up and down the hills, past the jazz bands playing in cafés, below the church's golden cupolas – where the elderly paused to kiss every cross and every statue.

V. AZERBAIJAN

Day 36 – Tbilisi to Shamkir Reservoir

As we drove to the border with Azerbaijan, the land turned from lush to bare, the grass from tall to short, and then eventually into an expanse of red mud. We left Tbilisi with a feeling of being rushed, of not having had enough time to savour its cafés, its nightlife. But we had to keep moving east; our visa to enter Iran had a tight window that opened only a few days later.

The border crossing proved uncommonly smooth – the transition to the Azeri landscape much less so. Minarets, which had all but disappeared since Turkey, started to pierce the horizon's line again. And beyond the police checkpoint, a newly minted road opened ahead of us. Roundabouts to nowhere and endless stretches of street lamps were also in fashion. All strange sights after a week of slaloming on cracked roads. All signs of the country's new fortune, one spent hastily since the discovery of gas reserves in the Caspian Sea.

Baku was still a few hours' drive away so we agreed to reach it the next day. Shortly after the crossing, we took a random turn off the highway and into mud tracks coasting the fields, in search of a place to camp. We had spotted a large water reservoir in the distance and hoped to reach its shores. Behind the calm water, a ridge of soft red earth met the sunset's last rays.

Upon arrival, two immense shepherd dogs approached the car. They barred the road, with growls more akin to bears than dogs. But their wagging tails soon betrayed them, giving us no reason to be fearful. They seemed to guard a strip of land enclosed by tall shrubs and marked by a hut made of metal sheets – standing precariously in a garden of litter. A garden so densely covered with empty vodka bottles that it must have been years in the making. In the distance, two men on a dinghy rowed calmly towards us.

As soon as they landed ashore, Anran approached them and asked in Russian if we could camp there. The question made the two men laugh. They were returning from fishing, both dressed in green waders up to their chest, and with faces made mysterious by the shades of their caps. Once off the boat, one of the two emptied a net of the small fish they had caught, passing them on to what once may have been a table. The other cleaned the fish with quick moves, while the rest of us sat there and observed as night took over.

They offered to share their catch. A fire was lit under the base of an abandoned bed and the metal frame was used to hold a pan in which the fish were put to fry. After the oil had cooled off, we took turns to pick up the small fish with our hands. It was hard not to notice the number of fingers both men were missing.

The atmosphere turned friendly and the two men shared their names: Yakov and Pavel. Grateful they had split their small catch with us, we set out our camp chairs around the fire, took out some whiskey from the boot and offered to cook a meal. Yakov soon disappeared beyond the fire's light while on a camping stove I prepared a meal with the last remains of the supplies we had carried from Italy: bland spaghetti. An unworthy payback for what we had just received. But this did not seem to trouble Pavel, who swiftly accepted a portion, and for a short while returned nothing but affirmative grunts to Anran's attempts at making conversation.

Once Pavel placed his bowl on the ground, his answers finally started to gain ground, travelling one sentence further each time. His silences turned from end points to pauses; his expression became pensive. He told us he had been a truck driver in Siberia for many years, he had been to jail, and he had had a family and a wife. But in his descriptions, or in Anran's sporadic translations from Russian, the order of events did not seem to matter. What had been was so distant that any permutation of those events would not have mattered. The break was too big – it was not a linear past; it was more like a bulk called the past. Now he lived in a hut, far from everything, relying on nothing but the lake in front of him, impossible to find, unless by error. He would fish twice a day, once at dawn and once at dusk, drifting around in between. And this he had done for almost five years.

Anran translated in short sentences, broken by long pauses. He could not hide his surprise; at the elegance of Pavel's Russian, at the strangeness of his choice. Pavel stared at the fire, Anran at him, and Kaspar and I at Anran. We all wanted to know more. Where had he cut his fingers? Why had he been to jail? But we had learned to pick our questions carefully, and it was not long before we understood Pavel had tired of being interrogated.

Day 37 – Shamkir Reservoir to Baku

We unzipped the tent in the morning to find Pavel and Yakov fixing their nets by the shore after having been out to fish. The light outside had lost the evening's softness, making the dumping ground we had camped in much less pleasant to the eye. We joined them for breakfast and soon after packed up and said our goodbyes.

Our time in Azerbaijan adhered to a strict schedule of unusual encounters, paired by no apparent pattern other than peculiarity itself. On this day, the first among these would be with the country's president – Ilham Aliyev – or at least his waving hand.

On the road to Baku, not far from the top of a tall hill, we were met by a queue of cars. The owners all loitered outside, with the air of having accepted the prospect of a long wait. The road had been closed as the president was expected to drive through a crossing ahead. A local industry emerged spontaneously, with some selling chips and popcorn. All the while, a large crowd gathered at the front of the queue to watch the passage. But when the moment finally arrived, a colonnade of black cars simply sped through, disappointing most.

Once off the hill, the road crossed a field of wheat stretching as far as the eye could see. We stopped for lunch under the shade of a lonely tree, with not much left to eat other than some cheese and bread. From a distance, an old man moved towards us on foot. He carried a spade on his shoulder, a weight that made him stagger at each step and – on what was a warm spring day – he kept a black fur hat to cover his head, and probably his sight too.

At a stone's throw from us, he paused and started digging in an unmarked spot, making no sign or sound to acknowledge our presence. We stayed still, afraid of interrupting an act that seemed sacred to this man. After a series of slow and solemn movements, he stared into the distance, placed the spade on his shoulder and returned to where he had come from in silence.

And still more would follow. As we drove through a town, a James Dean lookalike – with a leather jacket, hair slicked back and all – winked at us with nonchalance at a traffic light. In a nearby town, another man honked wildly as if to signal an emergency. He would not stop until we agreed to follow his car, which we did to the backyard of a school. Once out of the car, we discovered what all the urgency had been for: he wanted to take a selfie with us.

Baku's traffic swallowed us gently in its mechanisms, leaving us to gaze at the city's wealth: the loud roars of sports cars, the glass buildings of all sizes. Where signs of slums still appeared, cranes were nearby, intent on eating them away. Only a few Soviet buildings and mosques seemed safe from the purge. And the more we approached the centre, the more the city had been made to look like Paris. It was plagiarism without disguise: entire blocks had been built with the same Parisian limestone and roof tiles. Even the street signs had been set in the style of Paris's distinctive dark-blue plaques.

Since the early 2000s, natural gas had placed Baku on the map and, with it, the Aliyev dynasty. Ilham Aliyev, and his father Heydar before him, had ruled the country since the Soviet era, favouring a dictatorial style at home while featuring in British tabloids for their spending extravaganzas in London and closeness to Europe's elite. In many ways, the Aliyevs reminded me of the Gaddafi family pre-Libyan Revolution: ruthless, ever-present and somehow uncontested.

And Baku, having always been a crossroad, was being redrawn to fit Aliyev's many identities. The quasi-feudal, the businesslike, the Islamic and the Soviet all in one place. A purgatory between

Russia, Iran and the West. Unsure, often unwilling, to let passers-by know its view on the directions to heaven and hell.

Day 38 – Baku

In the morning, we walked to the National Academy of Science where we were due to interview its president, erudite about the country's history. It was a task we were duly unprepared for, but one we embraced with an air of great seriousness, each wearing the one shirt we had packed, and carrying a microphone, tripod and notepad with us.

The interview was part of a deal we had with our sponsors: we would receive the names of people to interview and locations to visit – together with some money – and we would send back photographs and occasional writings. Later that day, we would walk to the city's new railway station as part of another such exchange. All in all, we were content with and often incredulous about this strange deal. But we also took good care to keep our tasks as subordinate as possible to the planning of our days. We did so for freedom of mind, but also to remain not much more than tourists. Foreign journalists were a category much less in favour on our route.

After the interview, we wandered back towards our hostel, stopping at a bar that caught our eye. In a cold basement, young men gathered to play dominoes and drink tea around a dozen tables. The atmosphere was that of a ritual, spoken mostly by the sound of dominoes crackling in the hands of players, all strictly in black leather jackets.

We sat at an empty table, trying to remember the rules of the game. Until Kaspar mentioned that something had started to worry him. While mindlessly scrolling through the pages of his passport, he had spotted that his Iranian visa stated 'Valid for entry via airport only'. We pulled out our phones in disbelief, wanting to find something online that would tell us such details would not matter. But not long after, we realised Kaspar was right: there was a risk he would not make it into Iran – at least not by land. We agreed Anran and I would drive to the border the following day, and Kaspar would fly the day after that from Baku to Tehran, where we would meet again. We agreed all of this calmly, as if the slow advance of dominoes on the table could have numbed our minds.

Day 39 – Baku to Astara

It felt strange to part ways. Together we had long glorified overland travel, the mystique of drawing an unbroken line on the earth separating Venice from Beijing. But I understood Kaspar had never fully bought into this romantic view of our journey. He saw no sacred cows or unwritten rules. What mattered to him was making it safely to Iran and, for that, he was probably the one most clinched to earth of the three.

The road to the border leaves the city via its port, the last bastion of concrete before a barren landscape opens to the country's southern tip. There, a beach town by the name of Astara is split in half by a stream marking the border. We took turns to drive and write up an article on the previous day's interview – a task we both disliked but which we had come to share on long drives.

Along the way, we paused to visit the Gobustan National Park, a rock formation famed for its prehistoric carvings and its mud volcanoes. Dozens of craters lie in close vicinity to each other, some the size of barrels, others the size of small ponds – each releasing the gas trapped beneath them with fart-like sounds. Two kids circled these hysterically, screaming with excitement at each spurt. Their parents had driven them from Ukraine in a camper van; my main recollection is how completely sunburnt they looked.

But what struck me the most in this desolated place was a girl. She sold tickets at the roadside booth marking the park's entrance. It was an odd sighting from afar, to see a slim figure barely fitting in a wooden booth – one similar to a coffin, abandoned up straight in the wide horizon.

The girl was more or less our age. She had a clay-like complexion and long dark hair, floating freely along her figure. Anran exchanged a few words in Russian. Her eyes moved quickly with curiosity; her smile remained wide, shyness making only its edges flicker. She seemed excited to see us. Maybe she had tired of spending her day alone; part of me thought she was happy to see people of her age. No matter the cause, we found her excitement contagious, and Anran and I were soon smiling too, incapable of saying anything; overtaken by the pleasure of feeling one is the cause of another's smile. On the way out, I honked to thank her and she waved happily, leaning her body outside the booth.

I had not spoken a word to the girl, but as we drove away, I asked Anran if he thought we would still find her there, to greet us with a smile, if we returned in five, or maybe ten years. The same way I had wondered whether we would still find the two fishermen Pavel and Yakov at the lake, or David and his family ready to welcome us for breakfast when entering Georgia.

Anran reminded me of a phrase David had used when we left his place. He had said something along the lines of: 'I do this for you because I know you would do the same if I came to visit your place'. And while he had faced the three of us when saying these words, he had not implied a direct exchange, at least not one between himself and us. After that meeting, our contact with David would have all but ended. The exchange he saw could only have been between himself and humanity.

I told Anran I was unlikely to be on the other end of David's exchange. He questioned my use of the word 'unlikely' – asking if I could think of a time when I had received strangers at my table the same way David had. In my defence, I argued I came from a city with too many tourists, a place where that exchange did not seem possible. I would not have had the time or space to host every David at my door, so I hosted none instead.

I came to realise that what I sought out the most from others when travelling was what I least could give others at home. So how many more cars would it take for the girl to stop smiling, for David to tire of that exchange?

But as we spoke, Anran wondered if the number of cars or tourists really mattered at all. What if the problem was not simply that the exchange was impractical, but that it was open-ended, too. David was happy to give the little he had, his drop of water in the proverbial sea, knowing that one day the water would lift and it would rain on land, maybe even his land. I had learned to live as an individual who gives and expects to gather immediately, even at the cost of breaking a cycle. A cycle that was still alive in this portion of land. Somehow.

Once in Astara, we found a motel comprised of a corridor with half a dozen rooms and a shared bathroom. The town was a parking lot for trucks and our motel one for truckers waiting to cross the border early the next morning. It was a seedy place, the kind with no bathroom lights and where one soon finds it is probably better that way.

The streets had the atmosphere of an abandoned place of passage and the town's main square was an immense concrete slab cracked open by time. Loud music travelled from behind the walls of what seemed like a school. Otherwise, the town was deserted, with no restaurants or cafés in which to waste time. The only dinner we could find was a few apples, nuts and yoghurts from a corner shop. We took all this back to the motel room, set out our sleeping bags above the dusty sheets and fell asleep in short order.

VI. IRAN

Day 40 – Astara to Tehran

The border was a fervent marketplace, with all the traits we had come to expect. Taxis awaited customers crossing on foot, men sat next to empty wheelbarrows ready to ferry goods across, and bystanders with stuffed leather jackets converted currencies with their backs to the border guards. Others still stretched out their arms at every car window, water and cigarettes to hand.

Two trucks separated us from the front of the queue. We had been cautioned to arrive by dawn; a few hours of additional sleep would have meant spending a day behind exhaust pipes, or even postponing the crossing to the following day.

During the wait, torpor slowly gave way to anxiety. The possibility of not making it through still existed, for a document could always be missing in the eyes of a callous officer. Preparing our documents to drive into Iran had taken months. All to obtain a 'carnet de passage': an odd yellow booklet which border guards took as proof we would not be selling the car.

When our turn arrived on the Azeri side, we were led to a hangar for inspection. The border guards knew how to play our fears in their favour. In Anran's translation from Russian, their line was straightforward: 'leave your alcohol with us, if we don't find it, the Iranians will, and they will not like that'.

As I left them a bottle of unfinished whiskey, they repeated the same line, this time asking for gold instead. Noticing my surprise, the youngest guard repeated 'gold, gold, gold' in English and faced me.

None materialised from our car. Weeks later, though, a whiskey bottle did. Kaspar had carefully hidden one in the boot as a precautionary measure, knowing that Anran and I would have abandoned it all, leaving none for times of need.

Once through, we waited in no man's land to be allowed into the Iranian checkpoint. Ayatollah Khomeini scrutinised newcomers from a poster hanging on a cement wall. His grave expression scared and excited me at the same time. Beneath him, two young soldiers guarded the entry. They had the complexions of adolescents, their army clothes showing no indication of their rank. After a while, they opened the gates and smiled as we passed by.

The checkpoint was a gigantic parking lot with buildings scattered throughout, each pierced by rows of windows staffed by clerks. Outside, dozens of men stood with no apparent sense of urgency. These men were the fixers, their sole purpose being that of making foreigners' lives easy, for a fee. The crowd assigned one to us and, within minutes, he was sitting in our car, directing us around the parking lot, taking our documents and leaving us with trails of paper.

Once we had gathered all the necessary stamps, the inspection began. A guard dressed in civilian clothes and with a thick moustache came towards us. As I opened the boot, he quickly lifted his hand to point to the books we carried: an ambitious catalogue of tomes amassing the dust of the same roads they described. The guard looked at each one, skimming through the pages from cover to cover, as if hoping to find forbidden leaflets hidden among the folds. He then ignored the rest of the car and welcomed us to Iran.

As the last gate opened, the sight of the road ahead released me from all my fears. I congratulated myself for the speedy crossing, daydreaming of returning home to patronise all fearmongers with a simple statement: 'travel is easy, trust me'.

The fixer waited outside the gate for his compensation. I handed over my newly converted Iranian rials with a smile; he reciprocated with a bigger one. Only a half-hour later I would realise the size of his smile had been directly proportional to my stupidity. Failing to understand the conversion rate from dollars to Iranian rials, I had paid him ten times more than planned. A generous tip the fixer felt no reason to question.

As was typical on the road, contentment was overtaken by its half-sibling, confusion. Road signs were mostly in Farsi, and few things could be bought with the comforting certainty of a fixed price. At gas pumps, negotiation was a prerequisite for exchange. Fuel itself was often cheaper than water. But diesel fuel, on which our car ran, was reserved for truck drivers and we had to rely on their friendliness to fill our tank. Anran would lead the negotiations, treasuring these small contests. I learned to keep a distance, as more often than not I seemed to weaken his strategies.

We drove all day. The route bordered the Caspian Sea at first, then turned inland into the Elburz Mountains. Potent rivers cut through the valleys, leaving scars of mud across the wet grass.

I had read of these lush places. To me these were *The Valleys of the Assassins*, as Freya Stark had titled her book of travels in the region. The assassins were the Nizari Ismailis: a Muslim sect that had managed a shapeless state of fortresses in Iran and Syria between the 11th and 13th centuries. From their fortresses, they terrorised the leaders of adjacent regions with targeted killings – until the Mongols put an end to their reign while en route to Europe.

On our way to Tehran, we were passing by what had been the capital of this state: the Alamut or the Mountain of the Assassins – a subject of many legends handed down from crusaders to modern orientalists. Famous among these is the one shared by Marco Polo, who tells of the 'old man of the mountain' or Ala ad-Din, a ruler of the Alamut. Ala ad-Din was said to attract young men to his stronghold: a paradise of food, women and hashish. Once drugged, these men would awake outside the walls of this paradise they had become enamoured with. The price to pay to be allowed back in was steep but straightforward: one had to follow the assassination orders of Ala ad-Din.

While alluring, these stories failed to do justice to the Nizari Ismailis. Alamut was also the home of a renowned library, a hedonistic paradise of sorts. One that the Mongols left no trace of. Only the view from the mountaintop of Alamut remained – one spacious enough to allow room for both imagination and doubt.

It was past midnight when we arrived in Tehran. Our solitary road was surrounded by streams of cars; slowly drip-feeding into the heart of the city. Having heard of Tehran's reputation for traffic and poor driving, we decided to leave our car at a parking lot near the airport for a few days. From there, a taxi driver took us to the cheapest hotel he knew.

The hotel was hidden in a back alley. The grease on its red carpets was translucent and a sweating man in a tank top slept under a fan, his head resting on the reception desk. We woke him up and hesitated for a few minutes. But hygiene concerns prevailed and we soon walked out into the empty streets of Tehran.

We first settled on the idea of finding some food and started wandering. A car stopped by; the young man driving lowered his window and asked in broken English what we were looking for. We must have looked out of place. He knew a hostel and offered us a ride. I was too tired to question kindness, and Anran never did. I fell asleep in the back seat as Anran chatted awkwardly in the front. The drive must have gone on for at least half an hour.

Our new friend left us in front of a door with no sign, and asked for nothing other than a selfie. It was a newly built hostel, with the smell of paint still strong. We left our shoes in a small courtyard and exchanged them for hospital-like sandals. We were then guided to a dark room crowded with people asleep in bunk beds. We unpacked quickly using our phone torches, getting a few groans in the process. Starving, we then rushed to the kitchen and took turns to guard the door while stealing cucumbers from the common fridge. We were broken and ecstatic.

An hour or so later, I heard Kaspar arrive and settle in the bed below me. We had all made it into Iran.

Day 41 – Tehran

In Tehran, the snow-capped peaks of the Elburz range form the backdrop to long avenues headed north. The same direction favoured by the wealthy, who in the early foothills take refuge in their views.

The city is renowned for its disorganised style or – more frankly – for effortlessly defining the word 'chaos'. A chaos that consumed us quickly, as if in need of our attention. We spent the morning trying to find our way out of the Bazaar, failing to make friends in the process, and by lunchtime we had already retreated to the hostel.

In the evening, we joined a group of fellow room-mates who were headed to watch a football game. Persepolis, an Iranian team, was playing against a Qatari one in the Asian Champions League. I had never been a football fan but the others were, so I ended up following them on to a train towards the stadium.

On the train, it took us a while to realise that we were surrounded by commuters, not football fans. But by the time we understood we were on the wrong train it was already too late. We were on an express, passing by the stadium but stopping only kilometres beyond, in the outskirts of Tehran.

In a similar state to ours were two soldiers sitting in our coach with their camouflaged attire. The shared misfortune made conversation instinctive, largely through hand gestures and expressions. Age was an easy one to mimic. They were both twenty-two, like the fingers they flashed, like ourselves. They had recently been conscripted. Their hands would often run past the length of their buzz cuts, still in disbelief. The same disbelief their faces showed when they understood that where we came from conscription had long been abandoned.

They were also outsiders in Tehran. They showed us pictures of their girlfriends on their phones, their respective engagement rings. We showed them the pictures of our families. While I scrolled through these, they asked me to stop at the picture of a lion I had taken on a safari the previous year. It was not the animal that surprised them, but the fact that I had had the fortune to travel to see it. We then took turns to laugh, point at each other and stare pensively. We played with their army caps, and imitated stadium choruses of 'Ooh'. They had all decided we would still somehow make it for the second half of the game.

As we approached our stop, the atmosphere turned from light to excited. We ran towards a bus – supposedly headed to the stadium. The choruses continued on the bus, now made louder by claps and drumming against the seats. Once there, we all started running again. The vibrations from the stadium carried us forward, through the open turnstiles and upwards, towards the stalls. I was the last one of the pack; I had fallen behind while taking pictures, wanting to record this strange series of events.

As I slowed my pace, a hand suddenly caught my shoulder, blocking me with its tight grip. I turned quickly. There was a soldier dressed in green. He pointed at my camera and then pointed towards a large tent nearby. I complained, pointing towards the crowd my friends had disappeared into. His grip did not loosen, so I followed him.

In the tent one of the soldiers spoke some English and made me understand that they wanted to see all my pictures. Cameras were not allowed in stadiums. I knew that they had just seen an unruly pack of foreigners, running through the open turnstiles, drunk with excitement.

They made me sit while they inspected my pictures, standing around me in a cramped semicircle. I was speechless, looking at their expressions, hoping not to see them turn. I had nothing to hide, but one never really knows what is worth hiding. The photographs started with shots taken outside one of Venice's last Carnival parties, and that was not promising.

I had been sitting there for less than a minute when, through the half-open tent, I saw my two new friends come towards me. They came in, said something to the other soldiers, which I guessed was along the lines of 'He is our friend'. I was handed my camera back, and quickly rushed out. Noticing I had disappeared, they had come back to find me, spotting me by chance. I repeated '*Merci, merci*', but they were already running towards the stalls. I could not have thanked them enough.

We watched the last minutes of the game, whistling and chanting, taking pictures with those sitting around us. When the game finished we walked out, staying close to each other, carried by the slow pouring of people. The roads were all blocked. Only motorbikes whizzed through.

It was time to part ways and I found myself teary-eyed. Emotion, exhaust gases, strong lights all at once. We shook hands as good friends and boarded a taxi. Our friends walked away in the distance. I had forgotten their names and we had not exchanged phone numbers. No matter the laughter, we all felt we would not be meeting again. There were no fake expectations, just a strange – courteous – realism in this goodbye.

Day 42 – Tehran

We visited the former US embassy. Seized during the 1979 revolution by a throng of students, it had since been transformed into a museum of hatred. Together with a collection anti-American paraphernalia, there was graffiti of bleeding doves, 'Down with the USA' slogans and a cadaverous Statue of Liberty all lined up in an orderly fashion. I felt the sense of familiarity of the previous night suddenly wane and one of extraneity take its place.

Was this reversal not foreseeable? After all, the Western way of describing Persia, and later Iran, was through contradictions. Herodotus's writings on Persia had schizophrenically veered between feelings of fascination and disdain. And contradictions still seemed everywhere in the present. There was the rush to Western modernisation for some, curbed by the call to Islam's roots for others. There was the libertarian life within one's home, and the public one of duties and constraints. Hospitality and intolerance, poetry and brutishness. All narrow and apparently exclusive paths.

I thought of Borges's famous short story about the cartographer drawing ever-growing maps. At first, his maps are small sheets, focusing on the borders and the few large cities in between. A small map of Iran would highlight its edges: the fundamentalists and the modernisers, ignoring the majority of Iranians in between. The cartographer then becomes dissatisfied with his map's simplifications and draws wider and wider ones, until eventually the edges of his drawing meet those of the territory described. A map of Iran, one that faithfully describes it, can only be Iran itself. A map is not the territory it describes, until it is. But then of what use is it?

I could not make sense of these conflicts. Having no map at all was dangerous, a map was partial by definition, and an infinite one was useless.

Day 43 – Tehran to Kashan

I could not wait to get back behind the wheel, to the road. Where I could fasten to my thoughts as they rode, distracted by the moving surroundings.

We boarded a bus headed back to the airport's parking lot. The bus consisted of two crowded benches – Anran found a spot on the back bench, Kaspar on the front one. I sat on the floor, with my back leaning on the driver's seat and my arms hugged around my bag. From there, I could observe the passengers' eyes and have them reciprocate. And so they all did, outnumbering me. All but two green ones. They stared outside, ignoring the quiet feast of encounters taking place inside.

She was probably our age, with a dark complexion and an aquiline nose. She wore a light-threaded black hijab and a dress harmoniously at one with it. Above all, her beauty was addictive. Cramped between the window and Kaspar, she seemed visibly annoyed, or simply uncomfortable, to have him beside her. She would curl towards the side and not once did her eyes turn towards me.

Iran on that day seemed like an archipelago of cities in a sea of rocks. We coasted Qom, the first island on our course. My knowledge of these places was bound by few words and stories. Qom, to my mind, was a major Islamic hub and had been the home of both Khomeini and Hassan-e Sabbah, the founder of the Nizari Ismailis. Kashan, our destination, was due south and promised to be of a less pious nature than Qom. Of this island, I had read of villas built as holiday homes for Persian kings, merchants and nobles. I knew nothing of the places in between.

On arrival, we found safe harbour in Kashan. A crowd of children surrounded our car with excitement as we parked.

Festoons composed of colourful paper triangles hung in the streets and the vibrations of distant loudspeakers seemed ever-present. The atmosphere was festive all around.

Our hostel consisted of three adjacent rooms furnished solely with carpets. We set out our sleeping bags on the floor next to two girls from Hong Kong and Sweden who had been travelling around Central Asia for months. There was also an Italian named Paolo who had completed our same adventure the previous year. Having since fallen for Iran, he had returned to its roads. It was an apt community, of the kind we had become accustomed to find in hostels. A humbling and reassuring reminder that we were not alone in our dreams.

Excited to have found a fellow Italian, Paolo joined us for dinner. He had arrived a few days prior and knew his way around – which he showed by occasionally waving to the shopkeepers enjoying the cool evening from their doorstep. He was a solo traveller, savouring his rhythms when he so desired, joining other parties when he did not. Proud of this freedom, he would often repeat the words 'my rhythms' with the confidence of a connoisseur.

He took us to a place where a thick soup was being served from a cauldron – a hearty meal that filled us for less than a dollar. With our soups at hand, we sat on the edge of a sidewalk, sharing our adventures, happy the day had given us none.

Day 44 – Kashan to Abyaneh

We spent the morning running errands. Kaspar woke up early and set out for a visit to the barber with the acquired nonchalance of a local. We then walked together through the bazaar, stocking up on food supplies for the next few days.

The bazaar was set on a colourful stage. Rows of stands and jute bags paraded nuts and electric fans, bananas and cigarettes, flowers and mattresses – all equals under a web of domes. The cast was varied too. Old men played backgammon on foldable tables. A baker leaned outside his shop, glad to escape the oven's heat for a brief moment. Crossing the stage hawkers looked around with curiosity, ready to launch their chases. We appeared in this spectacle a little at a time, taking breaks between acts in the empty porticos of the adjacent mosques.

On our way out of Kashan, an argument broke out in the car. Few and far between, these moments would usually start with a complaint and end quickly with a long silence. On this occasion, Anran's stinginess had angered Kaspar. Anran had a record of returning close to empty-handed when in charge of buying food to share. Because of this, Kaspar thought we lacked sufficient food for the night of camping ahead. I decided to back Kaspar and – with a flair for drama – suddenly double-parked the car facing a grocery store.

As I rushed inside the store, a curious appearance caught me off guard – that of a man, with the look of a prophet. His eyes were sunken, peeking through a mass of curly hair, ancient in its length and greyness. My eyes instinctively followed his walking stick down to his bare feet, grey below a well-kept white linen robe. The main incongruity though was not to do with how he looked, but how he looked in these surroundings. His robes were pure, while all around shelves overflowed with cans, detergents and other goods – each full of colour, each trying to leave a mark on a buyer.

Upon seeing me, the man laid his walking stick to one side and gently brought a hand towards me. As I moved forward to shake it, he hugged both his hands around mine. His left arm remained folded, holding a drawing board at the height of his chest. He showed this to me. There was a childlike drawing of a fish with an eye above it. He took a pen out of his satchel bag and wrote 'I love you' below the fish. He then unclipped the drawing and handed it to me, slowly repeating those three words.

In return, I offered to buy the cheese he had placed on the counter and, while doing so, I ordered some myself. The shopkeeper smiled. He then waved towards the counter, making me understand there was no need for me to pay at all, for his cheese or mine. I insisted with more gestures, acting out a confused expression. But neither seemed to know a word of English beyond the three that had just been pronounced.

I returned to the car and handed the cheese to Anran in the back seat. I then unfolded the sun visor above the driving wheel and attached there a drawing of a fish, an eye and a phrase I had longed to hear again.

We left the highway not long after, following a secondary road that climbed into the Karkas Mountains. At the heart of this range, Mount Karkas stood tall, with the village of Abyaneh at its feet. Red mud houses faced the sunrise and the ruins of an ancient fort in the east. No paths were large enough for a car to pass through, but most had canals carrying water to the orchards downhill.

Our guidebook recommended Abyaneh for being a place that 'fenced by isolation for centuries had blossomed with a rare beauty'. But as roads to Abyaneh had been paved, distance no longer seemed to protect it. Instead, the village had been fenced by the borders of a national park – borders far more porous than those of sheer isolation. Visitors like us had become more common, even unreasonably so at times.

Our visit may have been one of those times, for soon enough we were affected by tourists' typical hatred of their own kind. We cut the visit short and started searching for a place to camp along the gravel roads. Only the arrival of night-time forced us to stop from driving further.

Day 45 – Abyaneh to Isfahan

I was the first to wake, finding my nose surrounded by feet on both sides. That night it had been my turn to take the middle spot.

I stayed in a comatose state for a long while. When the sun climbed out from behind the mountains, the heat became quickly unbearable. But I did not move. A winter jacket, a woollen hat and a layer of drowsiness had me in their tight grip.

A distant crackling noise started lulling me. It took a few minutes for my mind to meet my ear. It was a car, approaching from a distance – unusual, given how far off-road we had driven the previous night. I unzipped the tent and stood on the roof outside.

It was a model from a past generation, with an elongated front and tail – azure coloured, like the sky above us that morning. It stopped just a few metres away and a middle-aged man came out.

He was wearing a black baseball cap and a nylon sweater. We shook hands. Short sentences in our respective languages followed in a hopeful survey for a common ground. All we found was the valley's silence – our respective strangeness in it.

He seemed calm and slightly amused. I was still unsure of what to think. He started pointing towards where the gravel path continued, where the mountain's embrace got tighter. We understood he was asking us to join him there. He then sat in his car and continued his slow ascent.

We cleared our campsite and joined him. Higher along the path, the landscape changed quickly. The tumbleweed became sparse and the valley spanned just a few metres from side to side. Beneath the tyres, a stream appeared as a glass-like layer covering the gravel, its light presence soon disappearing under a layer of moss.

Behind a turn, the valley ended in a circular patch of grass fenced by the mountain's steep walls and the pink wildflowers adorning them. The man awaited us in the sunshine of his high garden. He sat on the ground, facing a small square of loose bricks. Among these, a fire warmed a samovar.

We sat by him for a long time, filtering brief exchanges through a phrase book Anran always carried with him. His name was Basir. He had a son who worked for a tyre company – this we understood from a key-holder he gifted us. He was probably the mayor of a town nearby and what he was sharing with us was his weekly moment of solitude. He asked us many questions. We understood few. He settled with the fact that we had three different nationalities. That seemed to make him happy.

In large part though, we sat there in silence. We were calm, at ease, as if we had nowhere to go. Only a few echoes travelled through the valley to reach our patch. Basir seemed to describe these sounds as the courting rituals between birds.

Once out of the mountain roads, we returned on the highway to Isfahan. We were going to draw a 'U' across Iran – sinking southwards from Tehran to Persepolis and Shiraz. There, we would turn around to cross the Dasht-e Kavir desert, Mashhad and the northeastern border.

Day 46 – Isfahan

In the past weeks, we had stopped being surprised at hospitality and had almost come to expect it. This was until Isfahan, where all expectations came undone.

We had two quarrels with the locals. On the first occasion, we were about to settle a bill for a meal but the bill turned out to be exorbitant. The restaurant owner had decided that the menu we had ordered from was 'out of date' and that prices had tripled since print. Hearing this ingenious trick the three of us all started laughing. But that laughter was short-lived, for the restaurant owner would not budge, and we eventually agreed to pay.

Not long after, a second quarrel ensued in the reception of a hostel. On this occasion, we were also being asked to pay an exorbitant bill. This time, though, the hostel owner did not have to be as creative. We had made a foolish mistake: handing our dirty laundry for a wash without asking for the a price. Tired by the previous fight, we left half the amount owed on the counter and left for the streets, only to find the hostel owner rushing behind us, shouting 'Police, police!' in English.

I could not tell what linked these two incidents – was it bad luck or the Isfahanis' renowned stinginess? Does hospitality end where tourism blossoms? Whatever the answer, by lunchtime we found ourselves with a lighter wallet and in search of a new hostel.

Once settled, we used the remaining daylight to wander, looking to understand why this city was so deserving of praise. To the Iranians we had met on the way, Isfahan had no match. And on this point there seemed to be universal agreement. They all respected an unwritten decree, a humble one: travellers should be told they had not yet arrived. For to understand a Persian's pride, the destination was always elsewhere. Until Isfahan, that is.

In the 17th century, Shah Abbas the Great transferred the capital from Qazvin in the north to the more central city of Isfahan. Together with the move, he launched a grand refurbishment project – one that embraced both variety and scale in its vision. Artists and artisans from across the Persian Empire were brought to Isfahan to forge a home for the arts and commerce – bedfellows along much of the Silk Road.

While no longer a capital in name, Isfahan remains one in spirit. Only such grandeur can be reason for the Naqsh-e Jahan Square to exist. The square is a gigantic rectangle, large enough to host two mosques, a royal palace and a bazaar. A scale that is indisputably grand, but not designed to overwhelm. Below the square's arcades, space is left for a human scale to flourish;

shopkeepers have niches to sell from, and passers-by a place to rest or pray.

Arcades play a similar trick at the Khaju Bridge, where two floors are stacked on top of each other to dam the Zayanderud River. On the top floor, the arcades shield the sides of a wide passageway where a constant flow of people crosses the river on foot. On the lower floor, the flow is slower as each arcade is partly truncated by the river, becoming a shelter for people to rest or meet, lulled by the water and shaded from the sun.

We sat on the top floor, with our feet hanging above the river below. It was a warm spring day and many had gathered for a picnic among the blossoming trees on the riverbanks. At the height of the bridge, a crowd of men and women had entered the shallow waters, dragging kites back and forth.

From this viewpoint, I pulled out my telephoto lens to shoot portraits without being noticed. As I did so, Anran asked me to stop. He told me there was no point in shooting portraits of interesting faces without knowing their story. He wanted all three of us to stand up, greet and meet each person. I, like Kaspar, wanted to be invisible, leaving those around me exactly as I had found them.

There were hundreds of people. We could see conversations taking place, children screaming and drivers honking along the neighbouring road. But we could not hear any of this. All we could hear was the roaring sound of the water cascading below, muffling us all under its permanence.

Day 47 – Isfahan to Abadeh

Late in the morning, we set off on the road running away from Isfahan. The plan was to drive all day, heading south to the ruins of

Persepolis. Before dusk, we would set up camp in the site's parking lot. It was a transition day, which we hoped to see through without effort – for once, leaving our minds free to settle into the next day.

At around midday, the engine began a crescendo of metallic thumps, soon followed by the chassis' own tremors and finally resolved by a piercing thump. Without life, the car slid on the gravel bordering the road, heading towards its inevitable halt – a gesture we all identified as hostile to the easy mindlessness we had scheduled.

Time after time, I had kept the fear of this moment at bay. I had skimmed through a manual for mechanics, I had compulsively checked the oil – almost every day – and when driving I would hush the radio to listen to the engine.

Within minutes of theorising, we had exhausted our mechanical expertise. It was hard to escape the fact that as a team composed of two economists and a linguist, our chances of identifying the failure were scarce, and even scarcer those of fixing it.

We had stopped at the entrance to a town. A perfect midway point between our origin and destination. A place by the name of Abadeh – either overlooked or deemed unremarkable by our guidebooks.

Bystanders from a roadside restaurant had gathered in ferment. Seniority ranked their distances from us; younger men circled closer while older ones maintained their nonchalance from afar. All men, each one seemed to be putting forward a theory on the cause of our breakdown. One could see the enthusiasm in their gesticulations.

Aware of my audience, I nervously repeated a script – turn the key, pump the accelerator and hope that the electric whines of the starter engine awake a grumble of mechanical power.

A young man from the crowd approached us. He sneaked around the car, theatrically tilting his head to bring his ear closer to the car's body, looking for a diagnosis as if a doctor with a patient. I jumped off the seat to follow his beckoning signs. He was kneeling by the rear wheels of the car, pointing at the fuel tank. With gestures, and presumably verbally, he wanted me to understand that I should kneel next to him to listen. There was a symptom – a prolonged but fading electrical fizz. The problem had been identified – a beginner's mistake – we had put petrol in a car that runs on diesel.

The young man took control of the scene. After a brief moment of conflabs among those present, I was shuttled on to the back of a motorbike in what I hoped was a hunt for the cure. There were mechanics everywhere along the road; each specialised in a different line of business. The young man was an apprentice in one of the many. He was in his early twenties and his name was Amir.

We towed the car's corpse to Amir's garage and spent the afternoon waiting for a pump to drain the fuel tank through a straw. Amir added a degree of gravity to his role by wearing a high-visibility vest – hiding the reindeers swarming his short-sleeved Christmas jumper. A tattoo of a heart pierced by an arrow occasionally peeked from his left sleeve. Sitting on large oil canisters, we observed each other from the opposite sides of the garage. I fantasised about a girl for whom I would get such a tattoo. Amir was probably trying to understand how we had made it that far.

We took turns to wander around the truck carcasses and oil stains in the area – escaping the sweet scent of petrol and the few locals who paid us a visit. Most were disappointed by their inability to communicate with us, or by our inability to communicate with them. A father brought his child and proudly pushed him towards us. The child knew a few words of English – he spoke shyly and favoured 'yes' and 'no' replies.

By the time darkness started hiding our surroundings the car had been emptied and refilled. As the motor rumbled back to life, we all glanced around searching for each other's eyes – toasting to a shared relief. We then followed Amir to the back of the garage. A glass pane demarcated a small office littered with receipts and half-opened cardboard boxes. He could not hide a smile. A smile both too mischievous and friendly to imply that the formal gathering was occurring simply for us to settle the payment for his service. Amir checked that no one from outside was watching. He then stood on a stool and lifted a liquor bottle hidden atop a shelf. He passed it on to Anran, nodding as if to reassure him. We were to celebrate the victory through signs – words could not do it.

I would later discover that in the early 1930s Robert Byron had also stopped in Abadeh on his way to Persepolis. In *The Road to Oxiana*, he briefly describes Abadeh as a 'favoured village' whose 'inhabitants are prosperous'. More interestingly though, while we all felt satisfied with the transgressive pleasure of a single sip from Amir's contraband bottle, almost a century earlier, Byron and his friends had lawfully prided themselves with having 'drunk a bottle apiece'. After all, 'Persians, broad as their views on religion are, drink mainly for the sin of it and care little for the taste'.

Amir invited us to spend the night at his place. Releasing us from hesitation, Anran excitedly jumped on the back seat of our host's motorbike. Kaspar and I drove behind. We stopped to buy a bag of raw meat, which Amir paid for, not accepting a dime from us. We then left the asphalted road and followed a dirt track towards a lonesome light flickering in the distance.

A cement wall enclosed a well-kept vineyard and a one-room building with a portico. The structures were all unpainted, as if still under construction. Amir's father, an old man in a blazer, greeted us as we entered. He had a moustache and the ancient tan of those who spend their life under the sun.

Amir unrolled a wide carpet under the portico. He then pierced the meat on to the skewers and laid out a bowl of goat's milk yoghurt, onions and a stack of flatbread sprinkled with za'atar. We sat cross-legged at different corners of the carpet. Amir's father remained quiet, observant, as an unstable stack of ash grew on his cigarette. Since our arrival, he had never taken off two earphones. On his side, Kaspar sat at ease, chopping onions with his pocketknife. He looked up and smiled. I reciprocated, sending my eyes sideways to indicate the bare feet of Amir's father, whose toes were playfully feeling the bread.

A car entered the gates. It was one of Amir's brothers, a taxi driver. He had a full head of silver hair, matching a dirty white down jacket. Then another brother arrived, a police officer with a leather coat, and then another again, and another. Soon enough, we discovered that the quiet man sitting by our side had fifteen sons and daughters. Of these, it was only the men who had showed up for a dinner with the three stranded foreigners.

As if annoyed by the constant interruptions, Amir's father suddenly stood up and asked Anran to follow him outside the gates. Driven by curiosity, I joined them, leaving Kaspar behind.

We walked in the dark towards a prefabricated building guarded by two dogs. Amir's father hushed them and welcomed us inside. It was a room the size of a small container furnished with a portable radio, a few glasses on a dish rack, a samovar and a wool blanket spread on the carpeted floor.

Within seconds, Anran and I noticed that the blanket was moving and that a lock of black hair appeared from underneath it. The movements were followed by a sleepy groan, probably expressing annoyance at our presence. Who was she – was she Amir's mother or sister? And why had Amir's father decided to bring two strangers to disturb her sleep?

She did not show her face, nor did Amir's father say a word in response. He just turned on the radio, took off his earphones, and sat with his back against the wall, facing the open door. We sat closely, as he pulled out three glasses, poured some tea, swirled it in the glass and then threw it out of the door. Now that they were clean, he poured again and served.

After that, all three of us remained motionless. Amir's father was self-absorbed in a gentle trance, occasionally closing his eyes as his head undulated slowly, the only interruption being his occasional yells to silence the barking dogs outside. The songs on the radio had the taste of love, or so I thought. Male voices sang melancholically, pushing their notes to such heights that they could not be held long; trembling in a vibrato, their pitch held on to what was already lost.

After a while, and without fanfare, Amir's father stood up and left, expecting us to follow suit. Amir's brothers had all gone home. We laid our sleeping bags under the portico while Amir took out a blanket and stayed there with us overnight.

Day 48 – Abadeh to Persepolis

The next morning, Amir's sisters arrived en masse. They smiled shyly, standing in a tight formation they broke only to shake hands with us or to take pictures of the car. The encounter was expected to be brief, as their father soon summoned them outside the gates, leaving only one behind, by the name of Shaadi. She had been tasked with taking us around town, for she could speak some English and Amir had to return to work.

Shaadi had arrived with a carton of eggs, which she started cooking in the kitchenette, often turning away from the stoves to survey us, smiling every time. A thin layer of oiliness glazed her skin, radiating light from certain angles. Her hair was dark; like the lines of make-up circling her large eyes. Their whites and that of her constant smile overwhelmed us with attention.

It was only once we sat around a table to eat that she started speaking. She was a year older than we were and was studying law at university. Excitement carried her stream of words, which often overflowed into Farsi. Seeing our confused expressions, she would suddenly stop mid-sentence, as if to rest on the shores of her own stream. We could all feel her angst at not being understood, soon soaked up by waves of laughter, reliable for their constant return.

After breakfast, we started a tour of the fields. The father – still unnamed to us – led the way in his blazer. He proudly showed us a pool of cement built to store water and an unusually large mud structure nearby. Its contours brought to mind the architectural ambitions of a castle, but the walls, eaten away by the passage of time, did not surpass the height of our waists. We could not figure out its era or who had built it. Shaadi shunned our questions, running around its empty rooms, taking pictures of us. The father, who seemed to have a strong liking for Anran, had taken him hostage by the arm. He held on tightly to him until – as we left the structure – he lifted his arms towards the sky as if to say 'This is all mine'. Behind him, the tails of his blazer danced playfully with the wind.

After the walk, we finally said our goodbyes to this strange character and boarded Shaadi's grey Peugeot, headed to town. She drove with her window open, letting the wind blow on her white hijab at first, and her black hair soon after.

The town had few attractions so she treated us as one, placing us at the centre of her world, introducing us to all the friends she could find. Among these we met Farhid, a middle-aged family friend who spoke perfect English. He had left Iran for Sweden during the revolution and had returned decades later to retire in his home town. As is often the case, upon returning, he had found a town too different to recognise.

He took us to the abandoned villa of a wealthy family. Its walls were still frescoed. The family had also left Iran, but unlike him had never returned. Farhid could not bring himself to criticise the Islamic Republic. Instead, he preferred to repeat a subtle mantra: 'We need a new revolution'. One could not tell if he regretted more his escape or his return.

We bought Shaadi a bouquet of flowers to thank her for her warmth. She was ecstatic. A few moments later, I noticed Farhid whispering something in her ear. I could not say what he told her. Part of me feared he was telling her to be more careful in how she appeared in the streets with three foreigners. Then I hoped he had just said something along the lines of 'Hold on to this moment'.

At lunchtime, we all packed into Shaadi's Peugeot, dropped Farhid off at his place and headed to Shaadi's home: a gated villa on the edge of town. She lived there with her mother and two of her younger sisters. The rooms were bare of anything but carpets.

Upon arrival, we were asked to sit around a table; we were late for lunch and the soup was getting cold. Shaadi revealed her hair, and the two sisters followed her. The youngest sister wore big round glasses; she was an artist and wanted to speak loudly of her inclinations. The other had dyed her hair a blonde more forceful than her shy character. She rarely spoke but was visibly the most excited. The mother kept her hijab on, circled around the table and never took a seat. Under her glances, we ate quickly and mostly quietly.

After the meal, we moved to the living room. Two sofas faced each other, the sisters took one while Shaadi and the three of us sat tightly on the other. Silence was punctuated by occasional questions, and brief games of pronunciation of Farsi and English words. Then, a phrase that seemed like just another question pushed forward into the silence. Shaadi had started to sing. It was a lullaby, one she sang without accompaniment, with courage, repeating its few verses with a sadder and sadder tone. As she sang, the sisters let their backs fall towards the sofas, while the mother stood on the edge of the living room, not wanting to get too involved, but too curious to leave. Her frame was minuscule, her expression serious.

Out of courtesy, we were then asked to extend our stay. We refused with broad smiles for it all seemed strangely absurd. We had found ourselves on foot the previous night and now we were guests. Our fortune though was even greater than that – we had finally entered a private world, one we had long waited to see.

After we said our goodbyes, Shaadi drove us to the edge of town. We followed her to the point where the roundabouts ended and the highway began. She got out of her car, and as we were doing the same, she quickly waved before we could get close enough to hug her. We were in a public place and she was alone, so we waved back, honked and drove away.

For what felt like a long time we remained silent, revelling in our memories of the day. Then, without preambles, Kaspar asked a strange question: 'If something happened to Shaadi, would you try to help her?'

He knew we had all been thinking about her. And I knew he was not looking for an answer. What he was hoping for was a confirmation of having lived a shared experience, afraid a bug had caught him alone. It was not infatuation, or love at first sight, but an almost brotherly affection.

Day 49 – Persepolis to Yazd

We entered Persepolis just after dawn. At the top of a limestone staircase, two winged lions guarded the entrance to a natural terrace. Within a few hours, crowds and heat would conquer the site.

Persepolis was a prized catch. I had tasted the sounds of this name many times when reciting the journey's itinerary to those who chose – or were forced – to hear me dream aloud. Like the hiss of a snake, the last syllable is an onomatopoeia of the Orient. The name is so steeped in history that even the most exacting cynics could not resist being intoxicated by this sound of knowledgeability.

And Persepolis had certainly been a place of consequence. Darius I, also known as Darius the Great, made this city the masterpiece of his empire during the 5th century BC. Almost two centuries later, Alexander III of Macedon, who was also a bearer of 'the Great' denomination, would end this empire by burning and looting Persepolis. An act of spite – otherwise uncommon in Alexander's record – that was his way of exacting revenge on the Persians for having burned down Athens a century earlier.

In the 1970s, Mohammad Reza Pahlavi, Iran's shah, celebrated the 2,500th anniversary of the founding of this empire by staging one of history's most extravagant parties in the same city that had witnessed its demise. Luxuries abounded, as sixty heads of state, queens, kings and an emperor were hosted in a camp built out of kilometres of silk over a year-long period by French architects, interior decorators and couturiers. Fifty thousand songbirds were dispatched from Europe – only to die a few days later, muffled by the high temperatures. And for three days guests feasted on foie gras, crayfish mousse and Champagne sorbet.

This list of extravagances fed my imagination with amusement. For the shah, it was a recipe for disaster. By 1979, the outcries of the uninvited had become the chants of a revolution. The shah had attempted to legitimise his power by reviving the greatness of a bygone empire. He found not greatness, but a path to be gone.

We climbed further up along a hill, buttressed by Persepolis on one side. A set of tombs carved into the rock oversee the valley below, where remnants from different eras carpet the view. A light charcoal colour marks some of the city's marbles. Abandoned stage lights are the last remnants of an ill-conceived party.

Day 50 – Yazd

We all agreed to make Persepolis the southernmost point of our journey. Shiraz was only an hour's drive away, but moving further south had started to frighten us. Every kilometre that was not bringing us east, closer to our destination, felt like a risk. A risk of tiring our car, its mechanisms, and our luck. So after visiting Persepolis, we turned around to head north, towards Yazd. There, for a few dollars a night, we found a room in the basement of a hostel.

In the morning, we dozed for hours in the dark. Kaspar woke up feeling unwell and found some relief in the cool temperature of the underground room. His other cure – one we all shared that morning – was a recording Shaadi had sent us of her singing. We played it on repeat, our only worry being that we might tire of it too soon.

It was only in the afternoon that we finally walked out of our dungeon, headed for the streets of Yazd. I had heard a lot about this city. Marco Polo described it in his travels as the 'good and noble city of Yazd', a place famous for its textiles and for its strange wind towers. The towers he referred to still survive, capturing the breezes above the city's roofs to cool the houses below. To foreigners like us, these towers – tall above street level – were like lighthouses we could use to navigate in the city's labyrinth of corridors.

We had come to Yazd with the hope of seeing one of the last bastions of Zoroastrianism, Persia's major religion before Islam's conquest of the region. I thought of Zoroastrianism as one of the ancient roots of religion. Born probably around a thousand years before Christ, it slowly grew to become the official religion of Persia, branching out between Turkey and India. Its prophet Zarathustra exalted Ahura Mazda, the Lord of Wisdom. He taught that the world was formed by an eternal struggle between good and evil. A dichotomy that together with many other Zoroastrian teachings – from morality to monotheism – has left its traces in religions and mythologies dotted across the world.

But ubiquity is not always a synonym for success. Zoroastrianism had fallen far from its time as an official religion. Its remaining followers were dispersed in communities few and far between. Yazd was meant to be one such community.

We first visited a Zoroastrian fire temple. There, men dressed fully in white were tasked with keeping an ancient fire alive – the quintessential symbol of light's resistance against darkness. The fire sat in a pit behind a glass pane, with only a few logs feeding it at any one time. Legend has it that the fire was one of the last Atash Behrams – the most sacred type of Zoroastrian fire, brought together from sixteen different sources in a complex ritual. Some of these sources, we would later find out, included the fire from a baker's oven, from the house of a king and from a burning corpse.

At sunset, we drove to the edge of town to see the Zoroastrian dakhmas, often referred to as the Towers of Silence. Two hilltops were guarded from view by large concentric structures. Hidden inside each is an empty room with a tiled floor, open to the sky. Up to a few decades prior, the bodies of the dead would have been brought to these rooms for vultures and nature to clean. Once nothing but white bones remained, the purification would be deemed complete – the body having survived contamination from evil.

There was a solemn air to the place. Kaspar was ill but insisted on climbing the hill – a choice he regretted at the top as I saw him crouch in a corner. We sat there waiting for him to recover. Anran and I chatted about our wanderings of the day; to our disappointment, we had seen the rituals and symbols of this religion but had met none of its followers. Other than the men maintaining the fire, Zoroastrians had proven elusive. The sites were populated by tourists like ourselves, curious to experience these odd rituals and their air of magic – a word that itself comes from 'magi', the term used to refer to Zoroastrian priests. And while we all liked to think that that magic still had a life in the present, we could not tell whether in Yazd it had been sealed in the past.

Day 51 – Yazd to Kharanaq

We left Yazd to venture northeast. From there on, we were to become the spectators of a majestic play. A play on the varied forms of nothingness.

Our first stop was a Zoroastrian pilgrimage site named Chak Chak – or 'drip drip' – for its spring, perched in the desert's mountains. The site was only an hour or so away, but by the time we arrived, we were ready to heave a sigh of relief. Along the gravel roads, the heat had risen quickly together with our count of broken-down cars, until finally a green patch had appeared ahead of us, unannounced behind the curves of a serpentine valley.

A dozen houses and trees nested high on a cliff, overlooking the harsh landscape below. Where the winding road narrowed into steps, we parked our car. Kaspar was still feeling unwell and remained there to sleep, so we took the precaution of placing stones behind every tyre to block them from slipping downhill.

Once the motor died out, the site turned eerily quiet. The only person around was a man sitting under the thin shadow of a cypress tree. Dressed in white, he sold tickets to visit the shrine that gave the cluster its name and purpose.

The walls of a cave protect the shrine. Inside, an eternal fire is kept alive in a steel pit positioned above the spring. Legend has it that in the 7th century before Christ, Nikbanou, the daughter of a Persian ruler, had arrived at this mountain while escaping from an Arab invasion. There she prayed to the Zoroastrian god, Ahura Mazda, to protect her. Upon hearing these prayers, the mountain opened up, sheltering her in its bosom. The water is said to come from the mountain's tears, weeping for Nikbanou to this day.

Around the shrine, the site appeared to have a single inhabitant but space for many more. I had read that at certain times of the year hundreds of pilgrims gathered here from places as far away as India. I searched in every room, wanting to find someone, or something, to help me imagine these scenes. The buildings had no doors and the rooms were all bare. The only traces of a human presence were on the floors, blackened by fire – a source of warmth in the cold desert nights. Around these traces, no coal or wood had been left behind, for in the desert none could be found.

The road then took us to Kharanaq, where a gas station and a few modern buildings hide an ancient beauty from the eyes of those driving by. Behind this veil, a valley opens up below and, in its silence, an abandoned town lies at rest. Crumbling mud-brick buildings swarm the descent. A labyrinth for our curiosity to rush into, down the empty streets closing into dark passageways, upstairs to rooms with ceilings left open to the sky.

Close to its trough, the valley's slope falls steeply, forming a canyon where the earth softens. The riverbed is barren – its dry state being the apparent cause for the exodus from the town above. But the sound of water still freshens the air. Thin canals carry water from the new town to the fields opposite.

We joined a group of children playing by the water, hoping to wash the road's dust from our faces. Our condition must have been pitiful, for upon seeing us, the children's parents offered us a meal. We refused politely, standing on ceremony. The truth was that we were in a rush – the prospect of setting up camp in such a place excited us. And this truth must have been apparent, for they waved us farewell with a strange warning: beware of the wild goats roaming in the area at night.

Finally, we drove down to the riverbed and set up camp on the sandy terrain, with the town on one side and the vaults of an aqueduct on the other. In the distance, the tiles of a blue-domed mosque shimmered against the mountains' earth tones. A dreamy backdrop in which Anran and I took pleasure in setting up a proper camp, for once complete with chairs, table and hammock.

I then started a fire, feeling uneasy at taking over a task that Kaspar relished with a certain compulsion. He would typically set out to collect wood as soon as I parked the car and, rain or shine, would find a way to light it. This time though, his quiet presence could only be felt in the tense curvature of the hammock. He lay there, without complaining or seeking attention, as was his style.

Anran and I then sat to read at different edges of our camp, occasionally lifting our heads to admire our workings. I daydreamed about the grandeur of expeditions of a past era, when a wealthy minority travelled with caravans of tents, beds, gramophones, china sets and other absurd possessions. I had seen a testimony of one such expedition in Persepolis where, on the edge of the site, a strange cluster of metallic carcasses were left to rust. There were tractor-like machines used to lift dirt, and train convoys used to transport it – forming an open-air museum of archaeologists' tools.

They had been abandoned there from the days when Ernst Herzfeld and Erich Schmidt had excavated Persepolis in the 1930s. The two had enlisted hundreds of people from the villages nearby to join their digging crew. And together with other bare necessities of such ventures, Herzfeld had travelled from Europe to Iran with his pet alongside him: a boar named Bulbul – Persian for 'nightingale'.

A few chairs and a table sufficed for me to feel like I had built a small kingdom, one that I could transport a few metres upstream or across a continent if I so desired. And in this kingdom's lightness, I saw another one's reach, where paths were never the same, and days were not for waiting. This was the kingdom of memories, and on the road, I felt like its king.

Day 52 – Kharanaq to Garmeh

I was pleased to hear Kaspar's voice again in the morning. Excited by his recovery, we packed up quickly and headed towards the Dasht-e Kavir desert.

After just a few hours of driving, we entered the doors to this desert – in our map's view at least. In our view, the entrance was barely discernible. A constant scenery had accompanied us from the day we had first ventured south of Tehran, indifferent to the distance we had put behind us. A flat expanse of gravel usually stretched from both sides of the road; a canvas for daylight's studies of earth's red shades, oftentimes blemished by white veins of limestone. On windy days, dust unsettled from the dry rock, lifting a dense fog. The electricity pylons flanking the road remained the sole markers of the passing of distance, as punctual as metronomes. When the wind quieted, the landscape stretched open again, only to be bound by chains of low-rise mountains, violently cutting through the gravel with their sharp angles. Rising from nowhere, these lines seemed like the product of a child's hand drawing on a blank sheet of paper.

Towns got sparser, and signs even more so. To find our way, we would try matching the crossroads labelled on the map with those we saw after leaving a town. Navigation though was more challenging than expected. Endless tracks disappeared into the desert; their uncertain nature repeatedly firing us into debates on which of these were likely to appear on our map.

We stopped to fill the tank at the last signposted gas station. Quieted by the heat, we contemplated the horizon in silence, with palm dates at hand. The melting sugar had moulded these into a sticky block, making them at one with the brick-shaped box in which we had carried them.

As we sat there, a white speck appeared in the mountains ahead of us. By the time it had reached the plain below, I could distinguish a man with a long headscarf, partly left free to float behind his back. His features were dark, and the wind revealed the shapes of his thin figure, walking straight towards us at a fast pace, carrying a large plastic tank. On arrival, he ignored our curious eyes, filled his tank with water and returned, without pause, into the plain and behind the mountains. As he faded in the distance, one could almost feel the call of the shade niched between the ridges, the attraction of hiding in its anonymity, its immovability. In a rush, the man had returned to a place where rushing had no meaning.

He could have been a shepherd or a recluse living behind the first corner in the distance. I liked to think he was a nomad, a Qashqai travelling north to escape the summer's coming heat with his herd. It was wishful thinking, I knew. It was a claim I would not have contemplated had I not before leaving stumbled upon Italo Calvino's memoirs of his travels through Iran in the 1970s. In an essay featured in *Collection of Sand*, Calvino tells of meeting these vanishing nomads not far from Persepolis. After having visited the site, his encounter with the Qashqai sparks a reflection on the disparities between a sedentary and a nomadic life. The author talks of how both sedentary and nomadic people seek immutability – in order, he claims, to escape death – and yet they do so in completely different ways. The first attempt to leave a mark of their existence in stone, a sign for future generations to remember. Nomads instead leave close to nothing behind;

they find immutability by tying themselves to the rhythms of the earth, to seasons and the movements of the sky above. Theirs is a way of living that defeats the end point of death via repetition, by becoming part of an eternal cycle.

At the end of his essay, when weighing up the two ways of living, Calvino realises that he struggles to pick a side. He can neither embrace the sedentary or nomadic life wholeheartedly. It struck me how maybe none of us can. For while we all bend to one side, not many rest there with conviction. Doubts, however small, and the aspiration to move, always linger in the mind.

Following a number of detours, by mid-afternoon we arrived in Garmeh – an oasis where we had planned to settle for a few days.

The mud-brick village was surrounded on all sides by a green patch of palm trees, perfectly fitting the contours of our expectations. What we could not have imagined was the eerie silence of the place – its narrow streets and arched passageways empty. The only sounds came from a pen facing one of the oasis's guesthouses. Within it resided a babel of animals ranging from rabbits to camels, cats and sheep, all hiding under the shade of the mud walls. All with the exception of the apparent ruler of the pack: a black goat beating its feet in an abandoned bathtub, with pride.

We had planned to stay in one of the village's guesthouses. When we arrived at reception, the owner asked us to follow him to a house nearby while he drove ahead on a motorbike. The streets narrowed and Anran started following the car on foot, knocking against the windows when I got too close to a wall. At one point, as

I reversed, a knock on the back door was immediately followed by a loud shriek. I stopped the car, and got out to find Anran holding his right forearm with his left hand, his face pale. He had knocked too late or I had stopped too late (a debate unresolved for the length of the journey). Either way, his arm had been squeezed between the wall and the car, taking on the indents of the latter at the height of his shoulder.

Panic ensued. Anran descended into uncharted shades of pale, repeatedly coming close to fainting while his fingertips felt the edges of the straight lines tattooed on his arm. We led him into the shade and with the help of our host attempted to ascertain if any bones had been broken. Still in pain, he lifted his arm horizontally, erasing with a simple gesture the nightmare scenario of a broken arm.

The return to normality was almost immediate. Kaspar rushed to the guesthouse's reception to ask for ice and sugar, hoping the latter would stop Anran from fainting. I returned to the driving seat, steering clear of the blame game that was likely to follow the smiles of relief.

Once in the house, I helped Anran lie down on a sofa, and rapidly introduced myself to our cohabitees. I had ignored them on my way into the living room, but as the urgency faded, I was left with the impression of having lacked good manners. An impression made worse by the discovery that five of our six cohabitees were all of the opposite sex and in their twenties.

Kaspar and I made our best efforts to make amends by joining the group around the kitchen table. Three of them were from France, travelling around Iran like ourselves. They were followed by a solo traveller from Ireland, who had fallen for one of them in a hostel in Yazd and had since been allowed to join their travel party. The remaining two were from Tehran, or at least they used to be. They had been living in the oasis for a number of years now – helping to manage the guesthouse, running yoga classes for the guests and watching foreign television series. The oasis was a place where they could live without hijabs, more freely. In the summer months, they would shut the guesthouse and move to a friend's place in the mountains near Tehran.

We soon exhausted the topic of where we were from and where we were going to. I tried to make conversation by talking about the elections in France, only a few days away. But France felt distant and no one really wanted to talk politics. Instead, the conversation shifted to our surroundings. We talked about the mint plants in the kitchen, the pistachios we were munching on, the yoghurt that was being fermented near the fridge. The atmosphere turned calm, so much so that I felt like I had not just arrived there for the first time. It was as if I had only been away for a short walk – one I had started and ended around that same table.

The place was an ideal refuge where we could rest for a few days. A mixture of mud and straw kept the house together, with a wall separating our courtyard from an alleyway. As one entered, the front half of the courtyard was dedicated to practical necessities, with water tanks, clothing racks and a squat toilet. The other half was slightly elevated and dedicated to stillness, with white curtains guarding linen sofas from the peak hours of warmth. The rooms surrounded this second half of the courtyard, with low ceilings and small wooden doors that never closed. Every cranny was assigned a candle, a potted plant or a hanging bead, all adding tremors to the air's stillness.

When the heat became bearable, Kaspar and I went out for a walk, driven by our usual impatience to map our surroundings upon arrival. We left Anran asleep on the sofa where he had been stationed since we had set foot in the house. Aware of his talents in socialising, we both knew that upon our return we would find him chatting in the kitchen, by then a close friend of all our cohabitees.

We walked through a settlement of abandoned houses, headed towards a red mountain at the edge of the oasis. Canals criss-crossed between the palm trees and the air was suddenly dense with life. Mosquitoes hysterically released the energy gathered in the hours of heat.

We then climbed higher along the mountain's flat slabs, stopping halfway below the top to contemplate the view. A half-moon of mountains shaded the oasis on one side and ahead the gravel desert extended into the blurred air of the horizon. We sat there, exalted by isolation and relieved that we had been lucky, once again.

Day 53 – Garmeh

For what felt like the first time in a while, we woke up the next morning without having to go anywhere. The nights were cold and the days required stillness. Our plan was to honour nature's request.

The truth was that exhaustion had caught up with us, and that Anran had also fallen ill, but we could not tell whether he was still suffering from the shock of the crash or from Kaspar's same bug. Either way, we all needed to rest. And that we did, each in a different corner of the living room, moving only to drink water and mint tea. In the afternoon, our cohabitees passed by, asking about our plans, and leaving confused by the fact that we had come to the desert to lie on sofas all day.

We only stood up around sunset, after being visited by Kian and Reza, two men who worked for the guesthouse and who had taken it upon themselves to show us around. The two were both in their early thirties, but did not share much else beyond age. Kian was the guesthouse's do-it-all. He had a long beard and a dark complexion, while his eyes were always hidden by sunglasses. Most of what he carried or wore hinted at some practical use, from the marsupial pouch hanging from his neck to the large pockets carpeting his clothes. Reza took on the role of the village's spiritual guide. He was clean-shaven and carefully polished, dressed in a white linen robe that gave him a priestly aura. As we walked around, he would lead, stopping to name every plant, rock or insect. Kian would stay a few metres behind, observing but rarely speaking.

Day 54 – Garmeh

Kian and Reza offered to take us to the dunes. We waited patiently for the afternoon to soften the heat before driving off in a small caravan of cars. They went ahead at full speed, their two Toyotas lifting a trail of dust for us to follow. They drove separately, for both had talked highly of the pleasures of driving in the dunes.

After about an hour, tongues of sand started to take form. The first few moved shyly into the gravel road, often caught off guard by the passing winds. These thin tongues turned into bumps, flanked by small dunes on each side. The road then faded as the imprints of our tyres became clearer. Soon enough, all that was straight became curved, leaving us with no firm bearings but the mountains in the distance. We had been in a desert for a number of days, but it was only then that we saw what we had expected.

We deflated our tyres to help the cars stay afloat in the sand and Kian cautioned us to never slow down. He lifted his hand towards the sky and quickly dropped it to point to a tall dune in front of him. 'Drive fast, follow the ridges and try not to flip,' he said.

All three rules turned out to be hard to follow. I drove hesitantly, often sinking the car on one side. Not seeing us tailing them, Kian and Reza would turn back, and effortlessly dig us out.

We stopped on the edge of a high plateau just before sunset; below, a rough sea was in repose. One could hear the whispers of beetles roaming on the sand. The trails of their footprints were long and straight, as if full of intent. Many of these trails met around the rare shrubs sticking out of the sand. On their branches, swarms of beetles found peace, resting like cocoons. They hung precariously as the wind swept them back and forth.

While I was mesmerised by these oscillations, the others set out a carpet, lit a fire and placed a samovar on its side. The sky's blue had just started to fade into dark. We waited for the first stars to appear before gathering around for tea.

Kian and Reza told us of the many times they had driven into the dunes: alone, with their wives or friends, sometimes staying out for weeks. More than the place we were in, though, Kian seemed to be enamoured by the Dasht-e Lut, Iran's southern desert – a place so inhospitable that even he could only visit twice a year. With pride, he told us that its sands had got closer to defeating Alexander the Great than most kings had. I told them that to me, the Dasht-e Lut was the desert whose edges were guarded by the ancient mud citadel of Bam. A place whose beauty I had first glimpsed as a child when watching the film based on Dino Buzzati's novel – *The Tartar Steppe* – shot in Bam. A place we had decided not to visit, for it had all but fallen to rubble after an earthquake in the early 2000s.

It seemed fitting to talk of *The Tartar Steppe*. In the story, a regiment of sentinels protects a castle on the edge of a desert, keenly waiting for an enemy to show up. As the years pass, the enemy never arrives, only signs of it. Meanwhile memories, and with it life, fade into the dullness of waiting.

For Kian and Reza it seemed like there were no good reasons to wait. Both had left their lives in Tehran to build homes in a place that allowed them to stay close to the dunes. There was no pride in how they told their story. Theirs was not an act of courage or defiance. They seemed to imply that the desert had carried them there, not that they had decided to come to it.

For a moment, I felt like I had stopped my waiting too. I had read somewhere that in travel we discover what it means to leave the wait behind, at least for a short while. We meet those who live in the places we have at one point dreamt of moving to, but waited. We are allowed to see all the paths we could have taken if only we had left the edge of the desert. We see the lives we could have lived, with no commitments. And some would say – because of that – that all we see is a mirage.

Day 55 – Garmeh

We extended our stay an extra night. Anran was recovering slowly and Garmeh seemed like the right place to let a routine set in. A pleasure we had all longed for.

Our rhythms – like our surroundings – were silent. Around noon, we would relocate from our beds to the courtyard, only to lie in a daze through the warmest hours. Patiently we would wait for the shadows' profiles to lengthen, allowing us to take cover on our short walk to the local store. From here, we would all return with an ice cream in hand and enough food for a meal or two. In the evenings we would drive, returning after dusk to dine with our new friends until late.

That day, we drove to the salt flats nearby: a mud base generously dressed with large grains of salt. Its peculiarity was in the shapes in which these grains gathered. Thick veins formed perfectly geometric polygons, which in turn joined up in an immense white mosaic extending far into the horizon.

It was here, as I felt the crackling salt beneath my feet, that I started to feel a strong cramp in my stomach. I asked Kaspar to drive me back. Once home, I rushed to the toilet and only got out half an hour later, crawling across the courtyard. I felt so empty of energy I could not stand.

After Kaspar and Anran, my turn had arrived too. I lay in bed vomiting through the night, occasionally groaning for the others to come to the room for company or to empty my bucket. The wood planks we called a door were largely decorative, allowing me to hear the voices in the kitchen. They chatted and laughed, then Reza played the guitar until late. I wanted nothing but to be there with them.

At one point Reza came to the room to feed me some herbal medicines, which I took without reservation. He blamed it all on the canned food we had been eating for too long. As we would later realise, it was not the canned food that had poisoned us, but another habit we had each adopted at different stages in the past week. In the mornings, we had each eaten an unwashed cucumber – typically self-congratulating ourselves on the healthy choice.

Weeks later, we would start using the metaphor of a roller coaster to think of our days in Iran, often assessing at which point of the ride we had found ourselves at any given time. On this ride, moments of calm were short intermissions. Otherwise, we had learned to shuttle between extremes of discomfort and self-satisfaction. And I – Kaspar and Anran never failed to remind me – when crawling out of the toilet on that day, had reached the lowest point of the ride.

Day 56 – Garmeh to Mashhad

By the time Garmeh let us free, Kaspar and Anran had both fully recovered. They carried me to the back seat, where I lay down still half-asleep – my eyes below the window's line of sight. The route to Mashhad, in the northeast of Iran, was our longest one-day drive. A record that allowed us to infringe our ruling not to drive at night: an unwritten rule we had motioned for our families' peace of mind. And also a rule we had become accustomed to disregard, as exhaustion would often win over caution, prompting lie-ins and minimal route planning.

But as we entered Mashhad, our headlights slowly faded, rendering us invisible on the dark motorway. A switch had melted, exhausted by the distance. Only the intermittent honking to signal our presence to neighbouring drivers revealed our furtive entrance into the city. The car – which by now had acquired human-like status in our imaginations – had acted as our families' enforcer.

Day 57 – Mashhad

We stayed at a place called Vali's hostel, described by our guidebook as a poorly lit basement thoroughly covered in carpets. It was also the cheapest place for foreigners on the market – the latter being our attribute of choice.

In the morning, Anran started a haggling contest with the owner, a worthy challenger given his side job as a carpet merchant. Kaspar and I headed into town, greeted by the second call to prayer of the day – a Hendrix-like concert of electric guitar sounds emerging from a creaky megaphone. I followed him from one café to the other, often finding myself staring blankly at the table, unable to converse, but sufficiently content to have moved beyond a comatose state.

A wide avenue studded with hotels, souvenir shops and eateries led to the city's holy shrine. The buildings' disorder was eclipsed by the even greater cacophony at street level. There were faces and garments from across the Middle East – a diversity not solely a product of tourism, but also of the city's status as a safe haven for refugees; whether Kurds leaving Turkey in their numerous diasporas, Turkmens escaping starvation under the Soviet Union or, more recently, Afghans crossing the border from their war-torn country.

While rarely on any route taken by Westerners, Mashhad was one of Islam's major pilgrimage sites. Born as a caravan stop along the Silk Road, it became the home of an immense shrine honouring Imam Reza, the eighth Shia Imam, who died there during his travels in the 9th century. Through time, the city's name evolved from Sanabad to Mashhad, which in Farsi translates as 'the place of martyrdom'. Religion and the shrine, rather than trade and a bazaar, became the city's centrepieces.

Trade though left its mark. The geographical advantage that had allowed for commerce often turned into a misfortune: the trade routes through Mashhad were the preferred path for nomadic invaders heading West. Over time, these invaders would adapt to the comforts of ageing in a city, only to be supplanted by the empire-building ambitions of other fearless nomads in an endless cycle of ransack and prosperity common across the Silk Road.

On the walk back to the hostel, a café caught my eye. It was plastered inside out with a laminate of fake wood. Sitting outside, young men sipped espressos. Inside, the owner greeted us with a broad smile and a finger pointed towards a shelf filled with colourful coffee bags. Every detail seemed well studied: his satin waistcoat, the vintage prints decorating the walls. He diligently presented one coffee bag at a time, spelling out their labels: 'Starbucks', 'Lavazza' and 'Ferrari', among others – all equally foreign to an Iranian ear.

A fine example of the Westernisation that conservatives so despised. To our eyes, Iran was a constant conflict between two opposites: modernity and conservatism, secularism and religion. Addicted to the simple elegance of dichotomies, wherever we looked, we saw two colours.

And yet, that day we saw the downside of this addiction. For a while we remained seated on a marble pediment, facing the gated entrance of Mashhad's shrine. We observed the crowds of pilgrims, mesmerised. Hijabs worn with jeans alternated with burqas, men with thawbs, beards and skullcaps walked alongside others who matched slim polos with aviator sunglasses. All levels of piety were on display. It was a varied spectacle hinting that Iran's reality, like colour, lies on a spectrum.

VII. TURKMENISTAN

Day 58 – Mashhad to Ashgabat

Cornered between two stans, I often felt the attraction of heading east towards Afghanistan, following the route taken by Robert Byron in the early 1930s from Mashhad to Herat, and many other writers who had traced my dreams of Central Asia. Afghanistan felt like the ultimate test for explorers – walking a thin line between welcoming beauty and avoiding evil. A trade-off between risk and reward that I was unprepared to take.

Instead, our route went north into Turkmenistan – a country known to us only for its eccentricities. First among these was the requirement to wash our car before entering Ashgabat, the capital awaiting just beyond the border. Police deemed dirty cars out of place in a capital on the edge of a desert country. We were ready to abide. Obtaining a visa had involved swallowing our freedoms to accept a fixed and time-limited itinerary, in prepaid hotels – all topped off by an on-board guide.

As we left Mashhad, a light layer of dust suffused the landscape's colours. The wind forced passers-by to squint, with their arms reaching out as shades for their eyes' length. A couple on a motorbike struck me; their clothes flapped tensely as they drove at the rear of a truck, close enough to have no braking distance – which to them was close enough to take cover from the dust's path.

The open horizon was slowly punctured by mountains as the road went from straight to winding, from sombre to lush, humid and finally wet. Within a few hours, we were up among the mountains in a patch of land enclosed by cities' names, yet itself nameless to us. We drove on through an ever-thickening fog, rummaging through our backpacks for layers of clothing that had lain untouched since the cold nights in Georgia.

The solitude along the road was in stark contrast with the bustle of Iran. We felt the absurdity of our presence in a place that otherwise seemed forgotten by the world. We were interrupting our surroundings' routine, and that excited us.

On the way out, Iran's border outpost was a gate manned by a single guard. Leaving was always easier than getting in; what did not change was that one still had to pay a fee.

Beyond no man's land, the Turkmen outpost proved far more elaborate. In a building designed in the shape of an airport terminal, men and women sat squatting, waiting for the guards to X-ray their belongings. We waited a few hours, anxious to face the car's inspection. In the battery compartment we had hidden two cartons of cigarettes purchased in Mashhad. None of us smoked, but online blogs suggested that cigarettes were eye-wateringly expensive in Turkmenistan and smuggling a few in was worth the risk. The then President Berdimuhamedow had all but banned smoking and the few cigarettes sold legally came at absurd prices, in small batches and strictly at dawn. At least that's what online blogs told us, although each one had a slightly different story.

Our fears turned out to be overblown. By the time an inspection officer followed us to the car park, a burst of heavy rain had come to our aid. The officer looked visibly bothered to be outside and only carried out a quick check of the boot. He then stamped our passports and waved us through the gates.

Our guide Maksat waited on foot on the other side, sheltered in a makeshift hut. As soon as he saw us, he came forward and replaced Kaspar in the front seat. He seemed a few years older than us and had the look of an army man, with a buzz cut and bear-like physique; muscular but in a laid-back, non-threatening way. His expression made it clear that he did not really want to be there, and the truth was we would have preferred not to have him either.

But given that circumstance was forcing us to spend five days together, both parties tried to ease into conversation. He asked about us, what we did and why we had come there. 'Students' was our short and safe resumé. When we asked about him, he took a long pause, rolled down the window and lit himself a cigarette. He then turned towards Anran and Kaspar in the back, involving them directly, and with a serious look asked: 'Have you brought any cigarettes with you?' We sold him a pack and he suggested we sell the rest by waiting for customers in the hotel's elevator (which we later did, in the space of minutes and for a tidy sum).

His opening line may as well have been: 'Rules are not for me', for the rest of his story flowed neatly from there. He spoke good English, having spent a year in Pakistan while in the army. His regiment had been sent there to train. Maksat did not get along with his Pakistani colleagues and his drinking habits led him into trouble. On paper both countries were equally Muslim, but Maksat thought the Pakistani were 'too Muslim and no fun'.

After having been kicked out of the army, his English helped him find work as a guide. He followed tourists for nine months a year – the government did not let enough tourists in for the job to continue year-round. For the remaining three months he returned to his home town in the western portion of the desert to herd his family's sheep. His wife and baby daughter also waited for him there; but his marriage was an arranged one and he did not show any fondness for home.

While he spoke, Maksat guided us down the mountains and towards Ashgabat. The border sat along an area with an unusual microclimate and within a few kilometres Turkmenistan showed its true colours, welcoming us under a blazing sun. The desert's emptiness surrounded Ashgabat from all sides.

From up high, the capital is nothing short of a freakish vision. A vision made of straight lines, perfect parallels and right angles – in no way challenged by reality's disorder. Entire avenues are lined with identical buildings, all perfectly white. Every one of them coated with marble; hundreds of blocks of ten-storey buildings. And lots of it is not just any marble, but precious marble coming all the way from Carrara in Italy. Rome is not the city with the most marble buildings in the world, Ashgabat is.

Once we got up close, order continued to reign; the city was barely audible. Avenues had six lanes but almost no cars running along them. Rows of cypress trees had recently been planted and fountains were always in sight, their gentle sound refreshing the air.

We had entered another dictatorship. By most accounts this was the most isolated and paranoid one on our route, holding odd records not just in the field of marble.

Following the country's independence from the Soviet Union in 1991, its former President Niyazov made a reputation for himself. He changed the names of months and days of the week to his liking. January turned into 'Turkmenbashi', or 'leader of the Turkmen people', which is how Niyazov referred to himself. One of the country's largest cities had a similar fate, losing its Russian name of Krasnovodsk for 'Turkmenbashi' too. In 2006, the country's first president died and was succeeded by his hand-picked successor, Berdimuhamedow, who reversed the name changes – for weeks and months only.

Brutal oppression and a good dose of sheer luck kept the regime alive. The country had exported gas since Soviet times, but it was only after its independence that some of the largest gas fields were discovered. One of these, Galkynysh, turned out to be the second largest in the world. This treasure trove financed its leaders' passions for the grandiose. It also allowed them to dispense small palliatives, such as free gas and salt for all.

Gas money, though, had not turned Ashgabat into a new Dubai. The economy was almost entirely state run and the marble façades were just that, façades. As tourists we could only peek inside to the extent that Maksat allowed. He did so in careful doses.

First, he took us to the basement of Ashgabat's bazaar, where a survival economy existed one floor below the official one. Below ground hawkers exchanged dollars for the local manat currency at an informal (and far more competitive) rate than the official money changers. Cigarettes and other Chinese goods smuggled in from the porous border in the north were on display.

Maksat then took us to our hotel, The Grand Turkmen, one of Ashgabat's few choices. Again, the external structure was almost worthy of its name but the interiors were from another era, long past their expiry date. There was no internet or phone network. And if one dug further, there was an even darker layer, one we wished we had missed entirely.

Maksat recommended we try the hotel's downstairs bar. The bar was really a club, with leather sofas, loud music, blue neon lights and all. But this was no ordinary club. There were far more women than men. These women were all scantily dressed, swarming the bar while the men on the sofas eyed them with interest. Every so often the men would beckon those they most desired. We sat in a quiet corner, and ordered the cheapest beer on the menu, convincing ourselves that one beer left us in the camp of observers rather than participants. None of the women approached us. They looked sad; many were young, beautiful. The men were boorish, squalid.

After a round, we left Maksat behind and headed back to our room. A woman from the bar tried to follow us in the elevator. We insisted we were not interested; in Russian Anran told her we were students. Acting disappointed, she disappeared behind the closing doors. The three of us then all looked at each other, thinking the same thing: should we have come here at all? Here not being the bar; here being Turkmenistan.

Day 59 – Ashgabat

Maksat left us to wander alone. The travel agency must have judged that Ashgabat posed few risks; the majority of people lingering on the streets were either police or men without uniforms but with walkie-talkies.

Ashgabat did not offer much in the realm of history; few attractions had survived a powerful earthquake in 1948. But Turkmen leaders had done their best to make up for that. We visited a flagpole that at one point had been the tallest in the world. There were various iterations of golden statues of leaders with or without their horses. The then President Berdimuhamedow had a particular liking for the country's Akhal-Teke breed and had even put in place a Ministry of Horse Breeding.

More than anything though, two sites were the centrepieces to this museum of the absurd. The first was the Turkmenbashi Ruhy mosque built by the country's first president, Niyazov, on the edge of the city. As expected, the mosque was immense, featured lots of gold, and had probably tried to break a few world records. But what really stood out was that on the mosque's walls verses from the Quran had been inscribed next to those of the *Ruhnama*, or the 'Book of the Soul': a two-volume epic on the Turkmen people written by Niyazov himself. The *Ruhnama* was given the same standing as Islam's most holy text. It came to no one's surprise that we were alone in the mosque.

The second site was also built by Niyazov, this time to celebrate the country's neutrality. The 75-metre Neutrality Monument was a tower held up by three legs, in many ways similar to a Soyuz rocket. An elevator brought us to an observation deck just below a twelve-metre gold statue of Niyazov.

Celebrating neutrality seemed odd, yet on second thoughts neutrality was at the core of Turkmenistan's standing in the world. The country knew to mind its own business; it had all the credentials to be a pariah state in the same league as North Korea, but by never sticking its neck out it escaped the bad press. To the world, Turkmenistan – like Azerbaijan – was in the business of selling gas, lots of it. What it did at home few knew. Neutrality also meant few cared to know.

Day 60 – Ashgabat to Darvaza

Every fifty kilometres the police stopped us at checkpoints to take pictures of our number plate. Maksat's responsibility, it turned out, was really to keep us within an approved itinerary when on the road. Straying from it would have allowed us to peek too far.

Yet by leaving Ashgabat we were already being allowed into a different country. For all the fountains and pruned gardens we had seen, Turkmenistan was first and foremost a desert. The sands of the Karakum covered almost seventy per cent of its surface. And the Karakum was not a postcard desert of large dunes and soft curves. It was an inhospitable land of bushes and windswept settlements, barely latched to the side of the road. Houses were simple blends of mud and corrugated steel, surrounded by herds of camels and sheep.

We were driving to Darvaza, or the 'Door to Hell', a gas crater midway through the Karakum. With a seventy-metre diameter, this crater had been on fire since the early 1970s, when a Soviet expedition saw its drilling rig collapse, eaten up by the soft terrain. As the story goes, Soviet engineers lit up the crater to limit the release of dangerous gases, hoping that soon enough the fire would die out of its own accord. The flames – large and small – still live on decades later.

We reached the crater after a half-day drive. Gas filled the air with its sweet stench, heat blurred the view. The only signs of life came from a campsite a Polish couple and their guide had put up nearby. With his usual aplomb, Maksat pointed to a hill a few hundred metres away and said, 'Camp there if you want to wake up without a headache.'

We followed his advice, lighting a fire and roasting vegetables while Maksat handed round the vodka. With darkness, the crater became more alive; its ethereal glow lonely in the cold desert night.

Day 61 – Darvaza to Mary

Turkmenistan only had one highway connecting its east to its west. It was an artery for humans to feed from. Along it, in even the most desolate landscapes, was a succession of settlement after settlement. We followed this highway back to Ashgabat, then headed north for Merv where we hoped to see a faint hint of the country's ancient history.

The oasis of Merv was first settled in prehistoric times. The location would prove to be an auspicious one: the oasis sat between the Turkmen desert and the Afghan mountains, a good resting point for merchants and armies alike. Legend has it that even Alexander the Great may have stopped in Merv; his commanders transformed the city into yet another Alexandria and blessed it with the title of provincial capital.

Over the centuries that followed, the city's status grew as it became the capital of one empire after another. Under the Sassanid, Arab and Seljuk empires the city prospered thanks to commerce and cosmopolitanism. Zoroastrians, Jews, Buddhists, Christians and Manicheans were said to coexist peacefully, and at its peak in the twelfth century the city may have counted somewhere between half a million and a million inhabitants – making it the largest city in the world.

But while Merv had the past of a great capital – one comparable to Rome or Isfahan – it had almost no ruins left to its name. The few sites left for us to visit included the mausoleum of a Seljuk ruler and two fortress-like structures built out of mud. The first was a beautifully geometric building, the second stood out for their large size and oddly corrugated walls. Both were like none I had seen before.

Otherwise, much of what we could learn about Merv had to be imagined from written accounts. And the last chapter of this history is not one for the faint-hearted. In 1221, the Mongol army reached the city's doors and within days razed its buildings to the ground. Its citizens – irrespective of age or sex – were massacred. Hundreds of thousands of bodies were left unburied. So little survived that Merv's history after 1221 is rarely given much more space than a footnote.

We did our visits and then killed time with beers and skewers in the nearby city of Mary. After a few of each, Maksat insisted we all go to a club. This time, he promised, the place would not be sleazy.

It was only 6pm but we decided to give him a chance. We had found it hard to engage with Turkmens, for few spoke English and only the older generation knew some Russian. The few people we had engaged with had been young people in Ashgabat wanting to take selfies with us and a drunk old man wanting to know if we liked the Russian President Putin. At the club we could give it a last try before leaving for Uzbekistan the next day.

The club turned out to be a curious place, curious in a good way. It was still light outside but inside everyone danced freely. Men and women stayed in separate little groups and to our relief were pretty much our age. The women all wore traditional attire: a bright red or green silk robe and a skullcap from which long hair braids fell. They danced to the same pop songs I knew, with the occasional Russian hit I had never heard of, but their interpretation of how to dance differed entirely from what I was used to. They undulated gently, much like a rope does when held from one end; their robes were tight against their bodies. Their hands rested on their thighs, unbothered by the genre's loud bangs. The men wore jeans and white shirts, and were visibly less at ease in their dance moves which – like ours – consisted mostly of small fits of boxing acts.

We had joined the dance floor in our own group of three, slowly shifting across to see every corner; exchanging curious stares with all. More often than not we were the first to break eye contact. We did not speak a word with anyone, yet we could not hold back our smiles and a few hours flew by in a brief moment. Then suddenly, the music died out, the lights went on and police officers flooded the dance floor. We looked around to see if others were as surprised as we were, but everyone just picked up their things and quietly walked outside as if the police were invisible. It was normal procedure; it was 10pm and the curfew had started.

VIII. UZBEKISTAN

Day 62 – Mary to Bukhara

Another country, another border, another day wasted doing paperwork. We said our goodbyes to Maksat and got ready to face all that.

There was something we had come to understand about border guards. It was not just that they had too much power and they could empty your suitcase or look at every picture in your camera. Border guards were lonely; their checkpoints were often in the middle of nowhere and few tourists travelled overland from one country to another. Extending the stay of those who did stop by was their – slightly sadistic – way of alleviating an otherwise boring day.

On this occasion, the border was a particularly desolate place and the Uzbek guards were a young bunch doing their mandatory army service. They took turns to interrogate us on whatever came to their mind: 'Do you like Napoleon?', 'How many words did Shakespeare write in his life?', 'Do you have ISIS videos on your phone?', 'Do you have girlfriends?'.

Once they had run out of questions, or our answers had become very dull, they took us to their commander who stamped our passports and let us on the road to Bukhara.

Day 63 – Bukhara

The cities along the ancient Silk Roads rose and fell following similar cycles. When regional peace allowed for commerce, they flourished. Wealth and openness allowed for madrasas, or religious schools, to be built and the cities soon became not just commercial hotspots but intellectual ones too.

Then every so often invaders upended this order, resetting the cycle. When the Mongol army moved into Central Asia in the 13th century, the cities of Bukhara, Khiva, Samarkand and Merv were all razed in short order, their populations massacred. Yet unlike Merv – where the cycle broke – the other three cities were all given a new lease of life. During the Pax Mongolica that followed they repopulated and rose again.

In Bukhara, most of the historic centre was from this latter era onwards. We spent the day walking freely through bazaars, mosques and madrasas, entering one courtyard after another; sometimes we found the silence of a lone tree, other times men playing dominoes. Some courtyards had decorative pools. There were no ticket offices or barriers and we could get lost over and over without anyone asking if we were allowed in.

The buildings were made out of kiln-dried bricks. Most had carefully proportioned vaults which repeated in patterns that pleased the eye. The structures were complex but delicate and that made them elegant. The clay walls were often decorated with colourful tiles; wood columns and doors were painstakingly ornamented. And above it all, the famous domes shone with their refreshing turquoise colour.

Day 64 – Bukhara to Samarkand

In Bukhara, I saw my readings on Central Asia come to life. Since an early age, one of my favourite books on the region had been *Across Central Asia*, a thick tome written by the Swiss diplomat Henri Moser in the 1880s. My dad had found a leather-bound copy in an antiquarian shop in Paris and I had since treated it as my most precious belonging, packing it safely whenever I moved home.

Moser's life had been one full of adventure; he had left his family's 'boring' watchmaking business to spend his life travelling eastward, making many friends along the way. In his writings, he described everything, from irrigation to education systems. Most of all though, it was not his stories that mesmerised me but the etchings he interspersed in their pages. There were hundreds of prints of the buildings he had seen and of all manner of people he'd met.

And it was not just Moser who had stopped in Bukhara. Marco Polo and his brothers had spent almost three years living there, waiting for a nearby war to settle before continuing on their route to China. Bukhara had also been the setting of many of the great espionage stories of the 19th century. As part of their Great Game, Russia and Britain had used spies to survey the region and build alliances. The British feared Russia wanted to take over India and took great care to understand how Russia behaved in what they saw as a buffer region.

In these stories, Bukhara was a dangerous place, one mostly inaccessible to non-Muslim travellers. In the 1830s, the Scottish Alexander Burnes travelled in disguise from Afghanistan to Bukhara, repeatedly changing clothes, accents and manners to better fit in along his route. His travelogue *Travels into Bokhara* thrilled the British public, shaping their image of the region at the time. Only a few years later, when Colonel Charles Stoddart from the East India Company attempted a similar trip, he would be imprisoned in a dungeon and, together with Captain Arthur Conolly, who attempted his rescue years later, was decapitated in public. The 1940s book *Eastern Approaches* by Fitzroy Maclean – a James Bond-like character who inspired Ian Fleming's novels – interweaved this violent story with that of his own adventures to Bukhara in Soviet times. Bukhara was again largely off limits to foreigners and Maclean playfully recounts how he found ways to hide his traces from Soviet agents by jumping on trucks or sleeping in parks.

A rogue expeditioner, Marco Polo, and a couple of spy stories provided my frames of reference for Bukhara. Long before I even came to know what orientalism was I had already fallen for its tricks. But once I did learn about it was I then meant to dismiss Moser's and Marco Polo's writings as orientalist fluff? Or was there still some historical value in them? I settled on the latter, mostly out of admiration for these characters. On espionage I was far more torn.

An espionage story could be just that: a story with spies. But beneath the surface one could find troublesome tropes. These stories relied on creating a specific landscape, an Orient where trickery, freewheeling characters and all things exotic were spotlighted. It was an appealing image, one that I knew not to turn a blind eye to, yet I also found hard to reckon with.

I had studied social science at university and much of my time had gone towards finding these tropes, breaking them down and being one step ahead of someone else's thinking. I had learned to be not just cynical, but more cynical than those around me; about everything, in an endless contest for moral righteousness. It worked well in essays or debates, but it taught me little of how I should think of this imaginary world for myself. After all I could not unread these stories which I had so enjoyed.

I enjoyed something but that enjoyment relied on a problematic set of notions, notions I was taught to analyse, break down, critique. Instead, what I wish I had been taught was how to strip away this fiction entirely, not with cynicism, though, not with complexity, but with lightness. Lightness, I thought, would come with understanding why something appealed to my instincts, with seeing what I had in front of me without hearing my mind speak. Only then could I find the primal beauty in the things I so liked. Seeing Bukhara with my own eyes felt like a step in that direction.

Day 65 – Samarkand

The previous evening we had covered the 300-kilometre stretch to Samarkand. The road followed a fertile plain where farmers had just started to plant cotton – or 'white gold' as Uzbeks sometimes referred to it.

Cotton was still the country's main cash crop, but production had suffered some heavy hits since its Soviet heyday. The first of these had been a slow burn. Cotton production relies heavily on water and in Uzbekistan much of it was pumped out of the Aral Sea in the northwest. By the late 1990s excessive consumption had all but dried out this body of water, which up to the 1960s had been the fourth-largest lake in the world. Droughts had since become more common and dust storms often lifted from this new desert.

The second hit had come more recently. In 2009 a number of international clothing brands decided to boycott Uzbek cotton after realising that the country's harvests depended heavily on the use of forced labour, often involving children too. Almost ten years later the boycott had not yet been lifted.

But Uzbekistan had started to reinvent itself in other ways. Unlike its resource-rich neighbours of Turkmenistan and Kazakhstan, Uzbekistan had never struck gold and lived off fewer natural resources. To make up for that, the country had opened itself to tourism. A process that was accelerated from 2016 onwards, when President Mirziyoyev succeeded Islam Karimov.

The arrival of this new president had been greeted by some with hope. Any change seemed like good change: Karimov had been in power since the country's independence in 1991, following the autocrat's rulebook to the letter. In practice though, the new president turned out to be a disappointment for the hopeful. While foreigners had had an easier time obtaining visas, Uzbekistan was still in no way closer to becoming a democracy.

In Samarkand, the signs of a tourist-driven reinvention were everywhere. Large areas had been razed to the ground to make way for new hotels. Dust filled the air while cranes and trucks busied the view. Immense Soviet-era hotels, which had hosted workers from across the Union, were being redone.

We found a hotel that was neither immense nor new. The rooms had dark-wood terraces overlooking an inner courtyard – a garden morphed into a junkyard where turtles and rabbits roamed free. Dusty compositions of textiles carpeted every inch of wall. We liked it nonetheless; the owner was friendly and made space for our car in the courtyard. That was enough for our peace of mind.

❖ ❖ ❖ ❖

Samarkand is the city most people associate with the ancient Silk Roads. After his visit, Marco Polo described it as 'a great and noble city' even as Samarkand was still reeling from the Mongol invasion. A new golden era was yet to start – one that would leave the most lasting trace.

Unlike in Turkmenistan where most statues are dedicated to modern presidents, in Uzbekistan the national hero and star of the roundabouts is the 14th-century conqueror Timur, also known as Tamerlane. Timur was born to a Turko-Mongol tribe south of Samarkand. His family shared some heritage with Gengis Khan and, like his distant relative had done before him, he rose quickly. His military talents turned him from a second-tier bandit to the leader of an army of tribes to the ruler of one of history's largest empires. He remained undefeated until his death, which reached him while en route to China where he hoped to overrule the Ming dynasty's first emperor. By this time, Timur had spent the best part of four decades leading armies from the Caucasus and Turkey to northern India, going as far as capturing Delhi.

Timur's thirst for war left a legacy of death, with some estimates saying as much as five per cent of the world's population may have died during his campaigns. His taste for violence though did not repel his love of the arts; Timur became a well-known patron, sparing the lives of artists and artisans and often deporting them to Samarkand, the capital of his empire.

Samarkand became a hodgepodge of styles: Islamic, Mongol, Persian and Indian. All the while a construction spree was put in train. Timur had an immense mosque dedicated to his wife – a structure so large that it was intended to hold all of Samarkand's population within it. And the city continued to blossom long after Timur's death, in a period that has come to be known as the Timurid Renaissance. Ulugh Beg, Timur's grandson, built the first of three madrasas in the city's main square, the Registan. His madrasa – whose portal was decorated with tiles in the shape of stars – became a major centre of astronomy and mathematics at the time.

Two more madrasas were added to the square in the 17th century, enclosing the view completely, mesmerising visitors in an immersion of colours and intricate geometric patterns. The Registan was a sight that surpassed all my expectations.

Seeing us in a state of awe, a guard approached us to offer a tour of the square's minarets, all for the price of a pack of cigarettes. He told us the blue tiles of one of the madrasa's domes had been replaced recently and were shinier than usual.

On second thoughts the whole square looked like it had been refurbished only a few days prior. As it turned out, that was not too far from the truth; Samarkand stood in an area prone to earthquakes and its main sites were rebuilt regularly. The guard answered our questions about all this candidly; he seemed in no way bothered and the truth was he could not understand what perplexed us about it. What mattered to him was that the square looked like it had when it was first built. He thought the government had done a good job.

Day 66 – Samarkand to Tashkent

In the morning we left for Tashkent, Uzbekistan's capital in the northwest. We drove slowly, hoping to save on fuel. The government was rationing diesel, and the only stuff available was sold in plastic bottles on the side of the road, often diluted with water. To avoid that concoction, we relied on a few canisters we had filled up in Turkmenistan – just enough to take us through to Kyrgyzstan.

Day 67 – Tashkent to Fergana Valley

Tashkent was not an appealing place. Here too violent earthquakes cleared the city all too often. But unlike in Samarkand, the most recent set of buildings included austere offices and Western-looking shopping malls, with restaurants selling everything from pizza to sushi.

The previous night we had stopped in a hostel at the edge of town, hoping to spend some time researching the next leg of our trip. To cross the Kyrgyz border and reach Osh we had to cut through Fergana – a valley awkwardly split between Uzbekistan, Tajikistan and Kyrgyzstan. Fergana was a place both fertile and rich in resources, but it was also one of the most densely populated areas in Central Asia; a patchwork of enclaves which did not always get along.

There was no simple explanation for these disagreements. The control of water was a common motive, but there were also others, such as uranium mining, ethnicity and Islamic radicalism – the latter having strengthened in Fergana since the fall of the Soviet Union.

These motives struck against each other, lighting up violence. In a 2005 demonstration in Andijan, a city in the Uzbek portion of Fergana, government forces shot at protesters, killing hundreds – maybe more than a thousand. The Uzbek government, keen to boost its credentials as a moderate force, argued that the protest was led by Islamic radicals. According to outside observers, the protests were directed at economic strife and the government's corruption. Five years later, new violent clashes took place in the Kyrgyz cities of Osh and Jalal-Abad – this time motivated by ethnic divisions. Hundreds died, Uzbek residents fled and the border between Uzbekistan and Kyrgyzstan was temporarily closed.

The border had since reopened but we still worried. As part of our research, we decided that Kaspar and I would read blog posts while Anran would call the British embassy. The blog posts were not promising; there were horror stories of all sorts from both the Uzbek and Kyrgyz sides. In 2000, four US climbers were abducted from the southern edge of the valley and held hostage by an Islamist militia.

After a while, Anran called us over and turned his speakerphone on; he had managed to get hold of someone from the embassy. We were put on the line with a man who seemed excited to answer our questions. At first, he ran us through the British government's official advice: 'Take care if you travel to the Fergana Valley, given the potential for tensions in the region.'

But he did not stop there; Fergana had quietened down and he'd cycled from Osh to Tashkent the previous summer with his wife. He then took a long pause and added, 'You guys should really stop reading online blogs; the valley is wonderful,' articulating that last word in the drawn-out way only the English do. We thanked him and decided to leave that same evening.

From Tashkent the road narrowed in the mountains. Terraced fields followed the length of the road; houses were built on a soft red earth – at the whim of landslides that everywhere scorched the view. The single-lane road we travelled on was itself barely held together by a small army of workers. They busied themselves as the mountains and a river below ate away at their repairs.

We moved slowly, not helped by police checkpoints intensifying and trucks moving more and more at a snail's pace as the cliffs got taller. As nightfall approached, we still had a long way to go to get to the border so we set out to find a campsite. After trying a few side roads, we found one that rose to an abandoned construction site, hidden from sight and surrounded by a melting tongue of snow. We set up camp here and started cooking, excited to be doing so for the first time since Iran.

A light rain started – the one thing we had not bothered to check about Fergana was the weather forecast. We set out a tarp and took cover.

The wind picked up as small gusts turned to a constant roar; no matter how hard we tried to ignore it, a storm was coming. Before we could finish cooking, a gust of wind ripped the tarp apart and capsized our cooking pot on to the floor. Our dinner was gone so we packed our things quickly and met inside the car, half-soaked and with our head torches flashing into each other's eyes.

The tension eased; we laughed at our great talent for the outdoors, at the ripped tarp in the car's trunk. It was an appropriate night to open the letters Kaspar's granddad Michael had handed us in Venice, each bearing the title: 'To be opened only in case of emergency, punctured tyre or extreme boredom'. Kaspar opened his first; it turned out to be a chocolate bar, partly melted but the tastiest substitute we could find for our lost dinner. We opened the other two letters too, celebrating each time at the sight of a chocolate wrapper.

Thunder started to echo in the valley like explosions. By the time we had moved to our sleeping bags on the car's rooftop, the tent shuddered and the car swayed from side to side like a ship. Separated from the storm by a thin foil, none of us could sleep. I kept imagining the worst scenarios possible: lightning hitting the car, a landslide or a flash flood carrying us down the mountain.

IX. KYRGYZSTAN

Day 68 – Fergana Valley to Osh

At first light we shook off from an unrestful daze and made a move for the border. The packing phase ended up being a disaster; we shuffled around chaotically under the rain trying to make sense of where we had left our things the previous night. We folded the tent leaving Anran's phone stuck inside. Then, while Kaspar changed into new clothes, I lost my temper with him for leaving the car's door open under the rain. Kaspar snapped back, saying he needed it that way; he added that I was being far too protective with the car.

After that, we drove in silence for a few hours – still half-asleep, still internally assessing why our fight had escalated so quickly. Anran occasionally threw in a remark to break the tension but neither of us was ready to follow up. Near the border, we spent our last Uzbek coins on three breakfast rolls and staggered through the checkpoint and its dreadful paperwork and finally into Osh.

Here we found a room in a detached house run by a shy girl in her twenties. She lived on the ground floor with her elderly mother. As we walked in and unlaced our boots, the mother greeted us with a broad smile from her wheelchair – she seemed genuinely pleased to have some company. Unfortunately, we provided none, collapsing instead in our room.

Day 69 – Osh

We opened our door to find the laundry we had dropped off in the wash had been dried, ironed and folded in neat piles; a gesture that did much to raise our spirits.

Once clean and well caffeinated, I took the propitious moment to apologise to Kaspar for the previous day's fight; he apologised back. The two of us had never fought before and we had reacted to this first time with shock, then statutory pride. Neither wanted this state to last a minute longer, neither wanted to be the first to end it. A perfect stalemate followed by a complete return to normality.

Osh was a peaceful city. It circled around a large market, one that was both a meeting spot – with pool tables set out between stalls for young people to linger around – and a place where knives could be sold next to flowers and toilet seats. More precisely, it was a market designed to serve the day-to-day needs of locals rather than of tourists' cameras.

On that day the city was celebrating Victory Day – the former Soviet republics' commemoration of Nazi Germany's defeat. Under a statue of Lenin, kids waved small Kyrgyz flags in unison while the Immortal Regiment walked past them and into a tree-lined avenue. The Immortal Regiment, as we had just found out, was a civil parade popular across the former Soviet republics. It involved people carrying placards with pictures of their ancestors who had died in battle or on the home front during World War II.

More than anything though, what caught my eye was the far less sombre parade taking place on the sidelines: observers of all ages standing by with an intricate panoply of headwear. Men wore white felt hats – also known as Ak-kalpak – with black patterns and folds; the height of each one seemingly correlated with the wearer's seniority. Some young women wore round red caps, others donned brown, red or green headscarves tied at the back. Older women favoured white ones tied around their chin. Unlike the Victory Day parade, though, this was all part of ordinary life; a system that hinted at social hierarchies and meanings at which I could only guess, knowing only how to admire the aesthetic.

Day 70 – Osh to Arslanbob

After a restful day in Osh, we started north for Arslanbob – a mountain village famed for having one of the largest walnut forests in the world. Legend has it that the first walnut may have been planted by Alexander the Great, a common story starter throughout much of Central Asia. The place is also considered sacred by Muslims, who claim that a disciple of prophet Muhammad planted the forest's first seed.

Once in Arslanbob I thought I understood why so many legends had piled up here; the landscape was overwhelming. And it was not the forest that did it for me, it was the mountains. Heavy with snow, their surface was alpine – steep and rocky – and that I recognised; what was new to me was their width. These mountains were far higher than those I was used to seeing in Europe, but that I could not assess – their peaks remained hidden behind the cloud cover. What I could see was their immense width and, grasping the simple logic that taller heights are typically carried by wider masses, I was left in awe.

This was our first encounter with the Tian Shan mountains, a range that crosses Uzbekistan, Kyrgyzstan, Kazakhstan and China; and whose name aptly means 'celestial mountains' in Chinese. Kyrgyzstan is the Tian Shan mountains in the same way that Turkmenistan is the Karakum desert.

While Arslanbob lived at a slow pace, in its people one could sense the buzzing energy common to base camps and places at the doorstep of adventure, of the wild. The main square was packed with men waiting to drive tourists up the trails in their 4x4 Ladas.

We followed one of these trails up to a group of waterfalls. Where the car could not go forward, we continued on foot, often alongside men climbing on horses – their destination in those empty mountains unclear to us. At night, we returned to town and found a guesthouse that consisted of a room with a fireplace and carpets for us to lay our sleeping bags on. Outside, the shower took its freezing water straight from a river and within a walled garden chickens and children roamed free – the children taking great pride in showing us how to use an axe to cut wood.

At dinner, we were told to wait on the floor by the fire. Arslanbob was mostly inhabited by Uzbeks, and the first dish we were brought was their famed bread. Uzbeks press metal stamps on glazed flatbread, leaving beautiful geometric patterns – each appropriate for a different circumstance, each equally ephemeral. After the bread, we then waited for the main; first an hour, then two. Just as we were about to set foot in our sleeping bags, the main finally arrived. It was a laghman, a pulled noodle broth with meat and vegetables that had been our staple food for some time now. What had taken so long? The chicken in our broth was one we had seen roaming in the garden not long before.

Day 71 – Arslanbob to somewhere near Son-Kul

Roads in Kyrgyzstan were scarce and to reach the capital Bishkek in the north we had to choose between two options. The first was to follow the country's main highway for a day's drive. The second took twice as long and involved mostly unpaved roads; its draw though was that it passed the Son-Kul lake – a 3,000-metre-high plateau where nomads were known to set up yurts for the summer.

It was not yet summer, but stunned by the pictures in our guidebook we took the second option anyhow and by the afternoon were high up in the mountains, approaching the lake. Along the road wild horses grazed on green slopes, with dozens of young ones having just been born that spring. Humans had disappeared from sight; the only signs of civilisation were the carcasses of abandoned buses that had somehow made it there and were now boarded up to be used as homes by nomads passing through.

Snow was melting from the peaks, forming streams large and small. It felt like a miracle that such a wet strip of gravel road even managed to hold on to the mountain. Towards the top of the pass, where snow had not melted, a narrow corridor had been cleared for the road to cut through. The walls of ice on each side were soon taller than our car.

In this corridor we drove on, with no sense of our surroundings until the odd sight of a yellow tractor appeared before us, blocking the road. A dozen or so Chinese workers were clearing the snow, grinding forward a few hundred metres a day. The problem was that they were not done; the pass was still closed and was due to open in exactly five days. Our only option now was to find a way to reverse on that tight corridor, drive hundreds of kilometres back to where we had come from and start again, this time taking the highway to Bishkek. All this without even seeing Son-Kul.

But first, as night was upon us and with it the cold, we found a clearing and set out our tent for the night.

Day 72 – Somewhere near Son-Kul to Toktogul

The road we had snubbed turned out to be just as breathtaking as the one we had chosen. A single-lane highway followed the emerald waters of the Naryn River across a red-earth canyon. The highway's only downside was that the police used it as a money-making operation; stopping us constantly, holding up our documents and asking for money. Most times, stalling long enough by their side tired them out and allowed us to leave without paying. On one occasion, feeling particularly smug, we handed them our expired library cards and attempted to drive on straight after. That was the one time we ended up having to pay.

Many checkpoints later, we reached a dam and the Toktogul reservoir it formed behind it. A dirt track took us to the pebble shores of this artificial lake, where we set up camp on a tongue of land that reached forward into the water.

As the cooling motor ticked in the background, Anran prepared his signature instant noodles while Kaspar and I sat in our camp chairs admiring the view, the moon rising behind the mountains. The setting sun had turned water into the colour of petrol, reflecting the day's last hues. Clay dunes on the edge of the shore had soft curves and orange veins. Where the earth rose further it became rocky and grey, then white with snow.

From one end of the lake, dark clouds moved towards us, and soon thunder appeared too. A storm was coming in, and the night was going to be a sleepless one.

Day 73 – Toktogul to Bishkek

The tent dried quickly under a warm sun while the car speakers played the mellow tunes of Seu Jorge. We went for a swim, then had honey and biscuits for breakfast. And the day could have gone on in that carefree way.

Except a swarm of midges decided against that. Under attack, we took cover in the car, killed those that had made it in and drove away.

As the highway rose to passes above 3,000 metres, midges still filled the air – and the car's windshield. Overloaded trucks, many with animals inside, moved at a walking pace. We overtook one after the other, with the constant fear that behind the next turn a pack of sheep would surprise us crossing the road.

After many close heart attacks, the mountains opened, releasing us into a lush valley of small houses and broad avenues which was Bishkek. Here we found a hostel with modern amenities and a large room of bunk beds, one we shared with a mixed crowd. There were Chinese tourists, a Kyrgyz student from the countryside who had come to take a university exam, and an Italian in his fifties named Massimo.

Day 74 – Bishkek

I was curious to know what brought Massimo to a hostel full of youngsters; our shared nationality gave me an extra reason to think

I could approach him at breakfast. He was uncommonly tall, with grizzled hair and a strong northern Italian accent. Reserved at first, he soon broke free, charging at once into his life story.

Until a year prior he had been a long-haul truck driver in Europe; a job he described as draining. When the time had come to retire, he found he had few roots, so instead of stopping he wandered on, keeping his methodic ways: his plan was to visit every country in the world and he only had a handful left to go.

He explained all this with a passport in his hands, pointing out that it was running out of pages for stamps – the third passport in the space of a year. He was so proud of this number, of his stamps, that it was hard not to think his goal had turned the world into a box-ticking exercise.

When I told him our story, he responded with nothing but a question: 'What are you planning to do with the car?'

It was a difficult one. In a few days, once in Kazakhstan, we would have no choice but to deal with it; driving a foreign car into China was near impossible. It involved paying an inordinate fee, getting an on-board guide and, worst of all, passing a Chinese driving licence exam at the border. We had given up hope altogether of driving there, agreeing instead to travel onwards by bus or train. For the car we had three options: shipping it back to Europe, leaving it in Kazakhstan and driving it back at a later stage or selling it. We ranked our preferences in that same order.

After hearing me out, Massimo added a fourth option: he was willing to drive the car back to Europe from Kazakhstan, but first he was going to have to tick off Tajikistan and Afghanistan from his list. He did not want any money; he would do it 'for pleasure'.

It was an interesting offer, on paper the best option. And yet there was something odd about taking it, handing the car keys to a man I had just met, who seemed so convincing and yet so compulsive. To avoid being tempted further, I got up and awkwardly ended our conversation saying we'd have to think about it. He smiled at me, then left me his phone number in case I changed my mind.

Walking around Bishkek we came to realise an odd aspect of travel. To foreigners, a country's political system is often out of mind, hard to discern in the immediate. Democracies, even of the feeble kind, had been uncommon on our route; Bishkek was the first capital of such a country since Tbilisi, the last thereafter. All five Central Asian countries counted themselves as republics, but in practice only Kyrgyzstan gave some meaning to the word.

Kyrgyzstan had problems of pervasive corruption and dissent was not always tolerated, but its people had a good track record of ousting presidents who had stayed in power too long, calling for elections. In the country's capital though, the air tasted no different for that, the people were no smilier.

What was visible was that the city was far poorer than Ashgabat and Tashkent – many of the buildings were still from the Soviet era. Roads were flanked by irrigation canals rather than shiny new offices. With even fewer natural resources than Uzbekistan, Kyrgyzstan has an economy almost fully dependent on agriculture, made hard by a mountainous terrain.

A country's wealth is apparent from the outset while, with the exception of extreme cases such as Turkmenistan, its political system remains less obvious to outsiders. Wealth is physical, politics is not always. In Bishkek nothing screamed that Kyrgyzstan was a democracy, but once we knew we started noticing things: newspaper stands were more common, statues of ruling presidents less so.

Beyond these rare hints, we had to speak to people, understand what was on their mind, not just what surrounded them. And for that more time was needed, certainly more than we had given it on our route.

Day 75 – Bishkek to Issyk-Kul

Driving due east of Bishkek we reached Issyk-Kul, a lake the size of a small sea with summer resorts flanking its sandy beaches. We were arriving a few weeks before the season started and could drive on the sand, setting up camp where we pleased. The water was perfectly clear, the day hot enough for a swim. At sunset Kaspar lay in a hammock between the beech trees, strumming a melody on his ukulele. Anran and I sat with our feet in the water, staring at the snow-covered peaks all around.

There and then a thought started ringing in my head. The memory of this moment, and of others like it, would become my freedom and my prison. It would remain with me, absorbing me in its views, in the smiles of those around me, in the light breeze on my face. Yet that same memory would also stir an endless yearning to move, to reach places that had the power to absorb me in that same way. Places mostly far from where I was likely to be in life. These memories would be like a scent I loved, a scent I could always imagine, reaching me from behind a door I could only so often cross.

X. KAZAKHSTAN

Day 76 – Issyk-Kul to Almaty

From Issyk-Kul, we made our way to the border with Kazakhstan, then to Almaty. The road passed by Karakol, an outpost for hiking types – some sunburnt and weary-eyed, having just returned from the mountains, others still clean and ecstatic.

In one of the town's grocery stores, the shopkeeper looked at us with confusion, not managing to place us among this bunch. He then asked quietly, 'Are you tourists or alpinists?'

Admitting to the former, we all felt strangely humiliated.

Day 77 – Almaty

Our first task in the morning was to change hostel. Arriving late at night, we had ended up in a shared room with a married Kazakh couple who had come from the countryside to visit a hospital. We had found the husband kneeled at his wife's bedside as she barely moved, taken by a high fever and a skin tone that charted unnaturally dark reds. It was a sad scene, one we thought best not to share longer.

The hostel we moved into functioned mostly as a student dormitory for Malaysian exchange students. It had a military feel, with rows of open showers and a constant smell of fried oil filling the corridors. What we liked about it was that it had a time café at the end of the road – a multistorey building where you paid by the hour. Once in, you could make use of its games or quiet areas to sit, make tea and read at all hours. It was a welcoming place, one we set out as a base to meet every time we split up.

The truth was that Almaty was far more welcoming than expected. On first impression, it was like any other glitzy city of the oil-rich kind, with roads still fresh with the smell of asphalt, countless fountains, behemoth malls and flashy cars parked outside. But after a day's pause our opinion changed. There was a large student community, which meant cafés were hip but affordable and youngsters met up in the streets in ways that would have been rare in Baku, and unheard of in Ashgabat.

Almaty was also visibly multicultural, with Russian, Central Asian and Chinese lineaments all within sight. The city's fortune had been born out of mass migrations. During World War II the Soviet Union had moved factories, universities and thousands of people from its exposed European front to Almaty in the safer interior.

In more recent times, the city owed its charm to another lucky occurrence. Following Kazakhstan's independence, Almaty was spared from becoming President Nursultan Nazarbayev's favoured playground. That fate fell to the smaller city of Astana, which he deemed more geographically central than Almaty and made the country's capital in 1997. The windswept Astana became an endless construction site for some of the world's most pretentious projects. A crown jewel that the president would later rename in his honour as Nur-Sultan. Out of his direct sight, Almaty remained Kazakhstan's largest city, its major commercial and cultural hub.

In Almaty we had no choice but to start sorting our car problem. We tried doing so by searching online for shipping companies, then splitting up to visit them and ask for quotes. The start was not a promising one; most addresses turned out to be wrong or of shell companies, often in tall apartment blocks.

That afternoon we met in the time café already distraught, on the edge of ringing up Massimo and asking him to drive the car back. We then decided to cheer each other up by visiting some more addresses together. One of these was likely to be our best shot: a shipping company with a proper website.

At the address we found a modern office, a receptionist willing to serve us coffee and all the gizmos that would have made any start-up proud; our hopes rose further. We were then led to a room to meet Artem and Yulia. Both were good-looking and at ease with their English; neither was likely to have reached thirty years of age. He was blond, blue-eyed and had a strong physique; she was tiny, with a bob haircut and a red satin blouse of the same colour as the company's logo. They listened to our story, making us feel like they were genuinely on our side without actually saying much.

Reality soon followed. Theirs was a shipping company for goods on pallets not cars. Upon hearing this, I pointed to the picture of a large truck behind them and insisted that a car could easily fit in one of those. I was wrong. But seeing my desperation they agreed to help. We followed them to their office where they started making calls to their competitors. They each tried a handful and only one seemed interested. He would meet us in two days.

After business was sorted, we chatted a bit longer. They showed us pictures: Artem of the motorbikes he owned, Yulia of her recent wedding to a high-school classmate. Our fortunes had turned and we were all the more chatty for it. It was only the constant ring of their work phones that brought us back to earth.

But, before we could leave, Yulia handed us her business card and asked we call the next morning.

Day 78 – Almaty

We gave Yulia a ring in the morning and that same evening she came to pick us up at the hostel. Her husband drove; he was a quiet man made to look older by the suit he wore. The three of us were only a few years younger than them, but sitting in the back of the car we felt like kids out of school, picked up by the adults on their way back from work. A dynamic we knowingly kept alive through the evening.

Our first destination was a hill famed for its views and amusement park. The two of them walked hand in hand, taking occasional pictures, while we ran restlessly around the rides. We then headed to dinner in a chalet nearby. Yulia was a wonderful host, she laughed wholeheartedly and seemed genuinely curious about our lives back home. She was also fond of her husband, who was far sterner than her – or maybe was put off by the presence of three other men his wife had asked him to meet.

Either way, we did not help our cause, accentuating his sternness with our gaffes. The first of these came from me: I asked him what he thought of the film *Borat*, a parody about a Kazakh journalist who visits the US for the first time. His expression turned cold. I repeated the question thinking he had not understood it, which he had; the film offended Kazakhs and he did not want to speak of it.

The second gaffe came from Anran who asked him about his job. The husband's response was 'I work with Apple', which Anran took as a mispronunciation of apples – after all Almaty was well known for its apples and locals prided themselves on that. When

Anran probed further about apple varieties, he was met by an even colder face than the one I had seen. The husband sold computers and phones, not – as the three of us had misunderstood – fruits.

Miraculously he still paid for our dinner and could not be convinced to do otherwise. He insisted we were 'guests in Kazakhstan' and even offered for the night to go on, taking us to a bar for drinks, then a club. By the time we returned to our bunk beds we were drunk to exhilaration, caught out by a strong mix of these people's friendliness, how out of their way they had gone for us and, yes, vodka.

Day 79 – Almaty

The time finally came to meet the one person who had given us some hope of shipping the car. We took a cab to an industrial complex on the outskirts of town where once through a tall wall we were greeted by a promising truck fleet. The owner was a Russian man called Igor: short, in a checked shirt and jeans, visibly stressed. He immediately made it clear he had bigger fish to fry. The walls of his office were covered by a decal of Venice's Grand Canal; he had earned a small fortune and he took his wife and kids there every year.

All this we learned after talking business. Igor spoke almost no English, so Anran translated the Russian for us. He had few inhibitions and negotiated the dirty way. At first, he told us he was no longer interested in our car; the border between the European Union and Belarus had become too hard to cross and he did not want to risk getting one of his trucks stuck there. Then, when he sensed he had pushed us far enough, he asked how much we were willing to pay – we lowballed, making him laugh. All the while, his phone kept ringing and he kept shouting at people on the other end, intimidating us as much as them.

We had few cards to play. Anran's translation slowed the pace of the negotiation allowing us to think and chat among ourselves, but what saved us was probably Igor's pity. For some reason he had taken a liking to us, and the back and forth had turned more personal. He asked about our favourite places in Venice, joked about Yulia's company and their attempt to make shipping look good; Anran asked about his kids. Then suddenly, he got up and said he'd take just a bit more than the lowball figure. We knew nothing about shipping but the figure seemed so little we all wondered whether we could even trust him at all. He explained we'd have to bring the car back in a few days; he'd take half the payment then and half at receipt. He then left the room and sent in his secretary with the paperwork.

Once we had signed everything, Igor took us out to town in his cream-coloured BMW. The car played Italian classics from the sixties – half of which I did not know, but I still acted as if I did for Igor's pleasure. He called his wife and had Anran speak to her awkwardly about Venice. He then took us to eat skewers and drink beer. Italian football monopolised the conversation, together with long silences and the occasional business call. Once again, we did not pay for dinner.

Days 80–83 – Almaty

In the days that followed Igor called us regularly. There were charges he had forgotten to account for and documents we had to sort out with a notary. We agreed to the latter but pushed back on paying more by using the 'a deal is a deal' adage – talk of honour worked well with Igor. What worked even better was not picking up his calls altogether.

Our time was otherwise free to be filled as we pleased. We came up with small tasks, from cleaning the car to going on long walks, writing postcards and eating an inordinate amount of cheese rolls from a nearby stand. The days were warm and long, the streets finally familiar.

One night, in the hostel's kitchen, we came across two Brits with whom we agreed to share a meal. Just out of art school, the two were spending a gap year in Central Asia; they were scruffy and energetic, both conscious of standing out in the room with their tattoos and painted hair. Like us, ecstatic with their new-found freedom to travel.

We started talking about our routes, then quickly veered into what was Britain's topic of the day: Brexit. It turned out the two had voted for Britain to leave the European Union, and not only did they want to leave, they also wanted to do so the 'hard way'. Britain, they argued, needed a 'clean break' and the then prime minister Theresa May was too willing to compromise with the European Union. A new leader was needed, someone like Boris Johnson – the then foreign secretary with whom they were almost enamoured. They described him as funny, well educated and, most of all, a rebel.

From our end all this seemed firstly wrong, then thrilling; we had trained our arguments against Brexit for the past two months. Now we could finally launch our attack. And so we began. Kaspar went forward with his usual argument that much of the campaign to leave the European Union had been built on lies and that it was intellectually lazy to believe these. Anran followed with another dig, arguing that Brexit was inherently in favour of closed borders, and anyone spending a gap year travelling would not be consistent with its aspirations. We tried everything: Brexit was bad for Britain's economy, it was bad for its union, it was bad for young people like us – most of whom had not even voted for it.

But the more arguments we set out, the more we realised we were approaching them the wrong way. Their values were similar to ours: they were not for closed borders; they had read about how Brexit could hurt Britain and they agreed with most of our points. They wanted Brexit and Boris Johnson not because they believed in their ideas, but because they believed in the type of change their ideas implied. It was radical change they wanted.

If we had tried to, the five of us could have agreed to reach the same distant end point, but our way of reaching it differed so much as to keep us poles apart in the present. Kaspar, Anran and I believed in slow change, in reforms building on reforms. We trusted the current order to work; they did not, preferring a violent shake-up of its foundations. A gamble – even if reckless – gave them greater hope of reaching that end point.

No logical argument explaining Brexit's evils would have changed their mind. For that we had to look backward, to understand why they mistrusted the current order so much. It was a conversation the three of us would return to long after this dinner; one that Kaspar's granddad Michael had hinted at on our first day, but that only now had we started to grapple with.

Michael had reminded us to quell our anger by cherishing the fact that we had the right passport and enough money to travel.

These two Brits had those too, and yet they still acted as if they had little to lose.

Day 84 – Almaty

When we finally had to ship the car, we all felt rested, ready to move into China with just a backpack. We were also sentimental, saluting each part of the car on what we thought would be our last drive.

It turned out not to be. A few kilometres from Igor's truck yard the car started spurting and dying, spurting and dying. Then an uphill killed it definitively, leaving us stuck in the midst of traffic. Almost 20,000 kilometres in, and the car abandoned us just a handful from its destination. We all repeated this fact in disbelief, too frustrated to start dealing with it, to acknowledge the honking all around us.

After we had tried and failed to restart the car, a man with an old Mercedes stopped by and kindly agreed to drag us to a gas station. We told him where we were headed and he happened to know Igor – a fact I found in no way reassuring. Soon enough Igor was there too, together with a tow truck. Igor must have felt our humiliation for he helped us make every step painless, not saying a word as we loaded the car and towed it away.

Day 85 – Almaty

The problem was easier to sort than expected; a fuse had blown and, once identified, could be replaced within seconds. We could try shipping the car once more.

Throughout our journey, Kaspar had insisted I fight my pessimism by repeating the phrase 'I was born lucky and will die lucky'. It was more of a prayer than a statement; it felt childish and I was far too superstitious to say any such thing. But upon seeing the car load on the truck I finally said it.

On that occasion, Kaspar turned out to be right. A month later – when back in Europe – I called a number and a half-hour later a postman showed up. He handed me the car keys and asked me to follow him to a parking lot.

XI. CHINA

Day 86 – Almaty to Urumqi

After days at a standstill, we could finally head east again. We left before dawn with a driver who agreed to take us to the border. From there, we hoped to reach Urumqi late at night – the whole journey being just shy of a thousand kilometres.

The border overlooked the city of Khorgas – a modern complex of skyscrapers, shopping malls and immense yellow cranes. In the space of a few years, China had transformed a desert landscape into the world's largest dry port; Khorgas was now a major hub for China's 'One Belt, One Road' initiative.

Khorgas's role in this initiative was to shorten the travel times for goods travelling between China and Europe. A dry port was needed because China and Kazakhstan had different railway gauges, which meant that containers headed west had to be transferred from a Chinese train on to a Kazakh one by using cranes. To make it to Europe, the same process had to happen again at the border between Belarus and Poland.

No matter the oddity of transferring containers from one train to another, Khorgas opened a new overland route, and overland travel was far faster than via sea. In early 2017, the first container had travelled via land from Yiwu, in western China, to London in eighteen days. By sea, a journey would typically take double that time.

The route promised to revolutionise China's access to European markets. And not just that, the first passenger routes were about to open between the Kazakh capital and Urumqi. Travellers would have to change train at the border but – while doing so – were promised access to cheap goods on the Chinese side; companies registered in Khorgas benefitted from the city's low taxes.

Our experience though was about to be less leisurely than anticipated. In Khorgas, not only were we entering China, we were also entering Xinjiang – a province where Western visitors were not welcome.

Xinjiang was China's largest province, one defined by tough landscapes and difficult relations with the rest of the country. The peaks of the Tian Shan, Kunlun and Altai ranges made the region hard to access, the sprawling Taklamakan desert made it hard to cross. And culturally Xinjiang had always differed from the rest of China. It was a largely Muslim enclave inhabited by Uyghurs – a Turkic ethnic group.

Throughout their history, the Uyghurs had come into conflict with China's rulers in the east. In the early 1930s, Xinjiang gained its independence, becoming the East Turkestan Republic. The Republic was short-lived, and even a second moment of independence in the 1940s was quashed within a few years.

But separatist movements lived on to this day. Occasional riots and terrorist attacks made China's stance towards Xinjiang harsher, and that harshness caused even more discontent. Fixated as it was with maintaining a tight national unity, the Communist Party had started an effort to constrain Islam and Uyghurs' cultural identity. Mosques and other historical sites were being torn down across the province.

The Communist Party was also putting in place a surveillance state. In recent years, foreign observers had accused the Party of arresting hundreds of thousands – maybe as many as one million – Uyghurs and incarcerating them in mass detention camps. In these camps, Uyghurs were said to undertake forced labour. NGOs also thought that the camps were being used to limit births, in an effort to demographically annihilate the Uyghur population. In parallel, the Party was encouraging mass migrations of Han people from the east, the goal being to make Uyghurs a minority in their own province.

While NGOs were calling it a 'cultural genocide', governments remained far more soft-spoken. China had shown its willingness to retaliate aggressively against all those who spoke out and the fear of being cut off from trade relations outweighed governments' ethical concerns.

From our end, we had read about all this beforehand. We knew journalists had struggled to visit Xinjiang; much of the evidence on detention camps had come from satellite imagery and interviews with Uyghurs who had left the country. Now we were about to get close, and reality is often harsher when seen with one's own eyes.

We started the usual ritual of crossing no man's land, passing checkpoints and handing out our papers. Barbed wire separated nothingness from nothingness – a border that appears even more absurd than one drawn along a river or mountain pass. It was our last border crossing; the desert temperatures of that spring day very different from those we had faced when entering Slovenia.

At the Chinese checkpoint we were split up into different rooms. There, three officers signalled I had to empty my backpack on to a table, before rummaging carefully through my toiletries and underwear. It seemed their intent was to humiliate rather than search for anything in particular. A feeling they confirmed by taking my phone and camera to scroll through my pictures – laughing as they went along.

The whole ordeal lasted a few hours. When we were finally let go, I threw my belongings into the backpack without order – desperately wanting to leave that room.

On the other end, we found a driver and an old lady who wanted to share a ride towards Urumqi. She was Uyghur but Anran could speak to her in Mandarin. She offered us dinner on the way and gave us her son's phone number. He was a law student in Urumqi and she thought we should try to meet him there.

The roads were perfect and only the constant police checkpoints slowed our way.

Day 87 – Urumqi

We had arrived in Urumqi late at night, at a time that was not clear to us. China had one time zone; all time was Beijing time. But Xinjiang and the Uyghurs went by their own time.

Either way, we lost track and woke up late. We then wandered around the city aimlessly, still weary-eyed.

On our walk we looked for traits of Central Asia. We found them on people's faces – Uyghur men had long beards and wore skullcaps – and on the flatbreads decorated with metal stamps. Architecturally though, Urumqi was modern in a soulless way. Historical buildings had been torn down to make room for high-rise cement towers. The city was also heavily militarised, with armoured vehicles waiting at the main waypoints, and barbed wire fencing off gas stations.

Wanting to understand something about all this, we texted the old lady's son. He responded immediately, inviting us to dinner with a friend of his.

The old lady's son spoke good English. Like others we had met, he had learned to speak it by watching TV. He was also a genial character and a passionate storyteller. Every so often, he would throw his arms around our shoulders and excitedly announce something along the lines of: 'Have I told you the knives story?'

His friend mostly sipped beers, with a worried smile.

The knives story ended up being one of the many he told to feed our appetite about Xinjiang. He thought Chinese people from the east considered Xinjiang to be a sort of Far West; they had often asked him to confirm all sorts of horror stories about Uyghurs. One of these was that Uyghurs were said to have a right to commit three killings in their life if using a knife. The only glimpse of truth in this story could be that Uyghurs were renowned knife craftsmen and a number of past terrorist attacks in Xinjiang had involved stabbings. It was a typical 'us' versus 'them' story, one with a darker tone than I was used to.

Much of what he told us was so outlandish that it became difficult to know what to believe. He spoke about his university, and how students were forced by professors to install an app on their phone so that their texts could be monitored. Most students also had GPS trackers installed on their car. Yet he spoke about all this very normally, without fear. His could have been courage, madness or a flair for drama. Whichever it was, we kept the conversation going by moving from dinner to a club.

We ended up in a in a glitzy place with a dance floor surrounded by low tables and sofas. A place that fit the script of a club in almost every way, except for one. A pop hit would alternate with a song in Uyghur, with mellow flute tunes reminding us of those we had heard in Konya at the dervish ceremony.

When the pop song played, everyone would rush to the dance floor. When the Uyghur song played, everyone would return to their sofas. No one dared to breach this order. During the waits, eyes searched for contact, increasing the excitement of meeting again on the dance floor, only minutes later.

Days 88–90 – Urumqi to Turpan

Kaspar and I came to a difficult realisation in China: we were dependent on Anran. In Central Asia we still had a car and that helped split responsibilities. Even though Anran did most of the talking with his Russian, Kaspar and I could try to compensate for his usefulness to the team by handling the car. In China, we lost the car and with it any semblance of balance.

We struggled to know what to pick from a menu that had no pictures and even more so what to order. But the problem became all too apparent when, for the first time on our trip, we had to board a train. That day we were headed to Turpan, an oasis on the northern edge of the Taklamakan desert. Knowing we could not even read a timetable, Anran playfully asked us: 'Why don't you try to do the ticket yourself?'

And as the days passed, Anran's tone became less and less playful. It was a severity Kaspar and I deserved, for we were often comfortable being chaperoned. In these instances, Anran would just say he needed an afternoon off, leaving the two of us to wander alone.

The train journey was chaotic. Loudspeakers made constant announcements, rendering it impossible to hold a thought for longer than a second. On the train, small regiments of police walked around with metal detectors, in search of who knows what. Passengers stopped by to take pictures of us.

We still had to get used to all this: a world where private spaces – whether physical or mental – were limited.

Things only calmed in Turpan. Outside the train's air-conditioned carriage, the heavy warmth of the desert quietened everything. Turpan was in the second-lowest depression on earth and held the record for being the warmest place in China. It was a dry, not unpleasant, type of heat, but one that still forced life to happen mostly after sunset.

Turpan was also a town with a human scale, one we cherished. Many of the buildings had just one floor and streets were spacious, often bordered by canals and rows of eucalyptus trees. Old men strolled around with portable radios and Uyghurs were visibly in the majority here.

Unlike in Urumqi, a number of historic sites were still standing. Among these we could visit the 18th-century Emin minaret, which towered over lush vineyards. Like much of Turpan, it was built with a combination of wood and mud bricks, its forty-metre height carved with beautiful floral and geometric patterns. The mosque on its side had an arched portal, designed in the same way as those we had seen in Uzbek madrasas.

A few kilometres away, the ruins of Jiaohe had also withstood the test of time, over two thousand years after the city's birth. Jiaohe had been a major stop on the ancient Silk Roads. Standing on a tall islet between two rivers, the city was entirely made of mud; with houses excavated in the hard ground, rather than built above it.

Towering cliffs served as natural walls, offering only two entry points to the city. But the Mongols had still managed to breach these, ending the city's life sometime in the 13th century. What they had not destroyed then, the arid climate had miraculously preserved since.

All around these sites, the landscape was densely green. Until one looked higher, towards the hills, where a dry earth corralled the oasis. Turpan had the fortune of being rich with underground water, which nurtured orchards and vineyards. Renowned across China, these vineyards were celebrated for their raisins, carefully dried in structures perched high on the hills nearby.

It was hard not to romanticise this oasis. One could almost picture the caravans arriving from the desert to see all this. And while our home was not a caravanserai but a hostel, we acted as if we had lived through a long crossing ourselves. Our room was simple, but there was coffee and a freezing conditioner – two amenities we had often missed in Central Asia. Surrounded by these comforts, we let a profound laziness seep in.

Day 91 – Turpan to Dunhuang

We started flirting with the idea of speeding up our return. It was not the allure of comfort that had grown stronger, but exhaustion that had started to take its toll. As hard as it was to admit, we were not made to live like nomads forever.

Occasionally one of us would count the days of travel it would take to get to Beijing in one go. Since the early 2000s, the Communist Party's 'Open up the West' initiative had connected the developed coastal regions to the much emptier remainder of the country. There was an impressive railway network, and one could board a high-speed train almost anywhere. But even at high speeds, the distances remained enormous and Beijing was at least a few days of travel away.

Exhaustion, combined with this realisation, sometimes made us slip into a self-absorbed – almost survivalist – state.

I was the first to fall into it. While on the train from Turpan to Dunhuang, I started using a pocketknife to peel a mango; I kept my head low, my eyes focused on getting as much flesh out of the fruit as I could. Once I was done with the knife, I took the stone towards my mouth, and ate away at it, as if a predator cleaning a bone. My hands were sticky, the table had a small orange puddle, and for all I know I may even have grunted.

When I had cleared the stone, I lifted my eyes and looked up to see Anran and Kaspar staring at me with concern. Anran asked: 'Are you OK?'

I saw myself from their side – glassy-eyed, like an animal caught in the headlights at night.

Still, we never sped up our return. That would have been too serious a decision and no one was in the mood for that. Instead, we fought exhaustion with another state: one of mild exhilaration.

We had made it to China, and we could not fully believe it ourselves. There were no more borders or car problems to think of, and Anran and Kaspar knew how to turn any prop into a cause for laughter. It was almost a form of hysteria; living our days wobbling with laughter, finally letting the lightness of summer set in.

Day 92 – Dunhuang

It took many trains and buses to finally reach the Mogao Caves. Sometimes known as the Caves of the Thousand Buddhas, they were among the Silk Road's most imposing sites. Hundreds of caves had been excavated into a cliff overlooking an oasis and the Taklamakan desert ahead.

The caves were from different eras, their construction spanning any time between the 4th and 14th centuries. They had been built as temples for Buddhist monks, with the oasis becoming a place of pilgrimage and a stop for caravans. Occasionally, wealthy families had also built these temples to extend their legacy. A plan that had worked out well for them; the area was abandoned around the time of the first Mongol dynasty, but the caves were sealed, and only reopened in the 20th century, many still intact.

There were caves of all sizes, some only a few metres wide and deep. Others cut through the whole cliff, almost forty metres in height. To enter, one had to wait for a guide to open a wooden door with a key. And once inside, a torch was needed to reveal the mural paintings and clay sculptures. Most caves centred around a sculpture of a reclining or cross-legged Buddha, often together with a group of bodhisattvas. Sometimes we would enter a cave and find ourselves surrounded by the menacing faces of warriors. The walls were painted with scenes of Buddhist sutras, landscapes or patterns – an immersive and intricate play of bright colours.

What made the caves so unique, though, was not only that they were a record of Buddhist history over a one-thousand-year period. Being in an oasis at the heart of a trade route, the caves also became a melting pot of styles. The Buddha statues in the more ancient caves had the realistic traits of the Gandhara style – a style born out of Greco-Roman and Indian influences. The later caves had more Chinese elements, with the Buddhas becoming less human in their expression and more minimalist in style.

The main testament to this variety was the so-called Library Cave, in which thousands of manuscripts had been found when the cave was first unsealed. Written on hemp, silk or paper scrolls, these manuscripts often came from a long way, with languages including Hebrew, Turkic and Sanskrit. Generations of avid collectors had saved everything here, from Chinese administrative documents to Hebrew prayers, maps of the world and texts on astronomy. The earliest printed book in the world – the Diamond Sutra – was also found in this pile. To our disappointment though, the Diamond Sutra was now in the British Library and most of the other manuscripts were spread across the world.

The site's main sin, though, was another. While access to the caves was heavily guarded, access to the oasis was altogether different; a tourist experience that was reminiscent of visiting a stadium. Enormous cement structures held cinemas inside and buses would take you everywhere on perfectly minted roads. At the visitor centre, loud music blasted throughout while dancers reinterpreted choreographies with no clear ties to the spirituality of the place.

Surrounded by all this, we had a constant feeling of being overwhelmed. We could not stop wondering what this magical oasis must have been like long ago. It was a nostalgia for a past we had not even known, a common bug among travellers.

What we could not see was the desert all around us. How it never changed, while changing constantly.

Days 93–94 – Dunhuang to Jiuquan

We stopped in Jiuquan, where the Great Wall reaches its western limit. It was a harsh and unwelcoming place, but a city had somehow sprung up – in part due to an iron-ore deposit nearby.

During the day, the streets were mostly quiet; small groups of old men played dominoes in the shade of cement buildings. There were rows and rows of these, all seemingly identical, and we spent much of our time losing our way, asking for directions and getting wide toothless grins back. Sometimes we would hear the fizzle of a radio coming from behind a corner, only to find a crowd of elderly people doing aerobics – a common sight across China.

But the streets only really came alive at sunset, when thousands of men in blue jumpsuits suddenly flooded the streets, returning home from the steel plant.

Days 95–96 – Jiuquan to Lanzhou

Kaspar and I found it hard to connect with people in China. Up to Central Asia, our tactic to start a conversation had been to name a football player, a famous song or national stereotype. The common ground was minimal, but with Anran's help, we had often managed to babble for a short while. Now our few hooks seemed blunted, and when we threw a bait, we received nothing but blank stares in return.

Anran instead was not easily put off. Not only did he speak the language, he also had a way of signalling his respect to whomever he spoke to. He was generous with his smiles and everything about China seemed to excite him in an almost nerdy way. Our journey into China was merely a prelude for him; once in Beijing, he had planned to stay a year or more to study here.

He would often rave about China's regional cuisines, while Kaspar and I followed him diligently to wherever he took us. Over the past days he had spoken with excitement about Lanzhou's beef noodle soup. So, when we reached the city, he wasted no time in taking us to its best joint. The dish consisted of a flavourful broth, with shaved beef, hand-pulled noodles, coriander and a touch of chilli oil. It was both delicious and cheap.

Lanzhou though mostly left its mark for another reason entirely. Within the space of a few hours, we had all fallen sick – coughing and with our noses congested – even as the temperature was pleasantly warm. Lanzhou was an average city by Chinese standards, but what we had failed to learn before arriving was that it held a troubling record: that of being one of the most polluted cities in the world. A title it had earned by being home to a large heavy industry in a valley that trapped pollution.

Our faces were constantly covered in a layer of grime. And to make things worse, the hostel we found was run by an alcoholic, proud of his many drunken nights with the guests and who would not take 'no' for an answer.

On our first night, not realising our feverish state, the owner decided to throw a solo impromptu party in a room next door. Kaspar got up from his bed, went into his room and, without saying a word, unplugged his speaker. To everyone's surprise, we slept peacefully after that.

Day 97 – Lanzhou to Labrang

It took us two days to leave Lanzhou. The real reason we had come here was not to eat noodles, but to find a way to reach the Labrang Monastery. While it was only a few hours away, the logistics proved tricky, with few buses taking the winding roads to the site.

At an elevation of almost 3,000 metres, the monastery was nestled in a narrow valley cut through by the Daxia River. The valley was so high that the surrounding peaks seemed but walkable hills. The air was thin and the clouds raced across the sky, providing only brief comfort from the sun's glaring light.

The monastery was a self-contained town in its own right, with a modern city hanging on its edge. Although outside Tibet, this was one of the six most important monasteries of Tibetan Buddhism. Founded in 1709, it had established itself as a university for monks, housing almost 4,000 at its peak before the Cultural Revolution. It was a place of learning but also one that had acquired a gruesome history, coming under violent attack from local Muslim warlords at the start of the 20th century and again during the Cultural Revolution.

Today, the monks living here had been capped at just shy of 1,800; many were children, holding their red tunics tight against the mountain breeze. They were part of the Gelug school of Buddhism, often known as the Yellow Hat School for the tall decorative headgear some could be seen wearing. It was a school that emphasised memorisation of its sacred texts, followed by a process of dialectical debate. A meditative life that unfolded in a complex system of courtyards, temples and sleeping quarters: one full of hidden entryways, rarely locked. Venturing through one door after another, we stumbled upon chanting men, a ceremony with dragon-masked dancers, children playing football and the fragrance of freshly baked bread coming from an oven.

The simple was in constant opposition with the intricate. White walls guarded interiors adorned with murals, statues and artefacts, with liberal use of gold. Dragons appeared along roof edges, and lion statues guarded the entryways of temples.

To an outsider, though, the most impressive feature was the so-called inner kora: a 3.5-kilometre path that pilgrims circled clockwise, edging around the borders of the monastery and marked by tall stupas at its main corners. Hundreds of prayer wheels lined its length for pilgrims to spin as they walked. These hexagonal wheels were made of inlaid wood, with meticulous paintings of patterns and sacred texts. They spun unpredictably, some slowly, others starting incessantly, but always soothing one's mind with each push.

Tibetans believed that the more challenging a pilgrimage, the greater the purification achieved. Along the path, many would prostrate themselves in front of each prayer wheel; they kneeled and slid their hands on wooden plates so that their whole body lay flat on the ground. Some pilgrims mumbled mantras, some could barely walk so they held on to the handles of the wheels to carry themselves forward. Heads were pressed against the walls in reverence, while insects were gently moved aside.

As dusk settled, the valley resonated with deep chants, accompanied by the solemn sound of Tibetan longhorns. A biting cold set in and we huddled with some monks around an impromptu show thrown by the town's drunkard.

The man had long hair and a ruined red tunic. He entertained the crowd with a speaker, singing songs with a raucous, inebriated voice. The monks all smiled but none laughed. Then suddenly a goat appeared, heading to the drunkard's donation basket. It greedily rushed its head into it, devouring the banknotes, then running away towards the hill as the drunkard chased it into the night. No one could hold their laughter now.

Day 98 – Labrang

The town had two hostels: one for tourists and one for Chinese visitors. The former was a dreadful place, with freezing water and dirty sheets, the latter was brand new. On the first night we had unsuccessfully begged to be let in with the locals but the owners complained they did not have a licence. We returned to the Chinese hostel in the morning and this time they must have pitied us enough, for they agreed to hide us in a back room.

We spent our day turning around the monastery, each taking a separate route. Our paces varied and we only reconvened in the evening, sitting on the mountainside at eye level with the soaring hawks. From here, the monastery looked like a picture maze, awaiting a skilled hand to draw a line towards its heart.

We could see the faces of the people below. A child monk skateboarded calmly in an open square, while nearby another stood reading in front of a doorway. Pilgrims arrived from afar with nothing but a small backpack, often barefoot, but always with a hat. The ladies wore colourful dresses and kept their hair braided, their skin darkened by the sun. Older pilgrims sat on the edges of the kora to chat and rest before setting out again.

None of us had spiritual inclinations but there was something deeply mystical about this place. And while we could not understand its symbols or meanings, there was something universal to it that reverberated in us. We could have stayed there for days, immersing ourselves in this magical realm, in a perpetual quest to unravel what enabled three sceptics to feel the meaning of sacredness.

Day 99 – Labrang to Lanzhou

We returned to Lanzhou and headed straight for the train station. From there, we took a night train for Xi'an, sleeping in rows of bunk beds that stretched across the entire carriage without doors or walls.

We slept with an eye open. Not so much because of the oddity of sleeping with strangers, but because we'd often wake up to find someone staring at us from the foot of our beds. Passers-by would stop and giggle, at times taking out their phones and creepily filming us trying to sleep.

Days 100–101 – Lanzhou to Xi'an

Xi'an was immense and, like much of urban China, it was everywhere under construction. I had read somewhere that China consumed as much cement in just three years of the 2010s as the United States had in all of the 20th century. It was urbanisation at breakneck speed, a metropolis still in the making among the cranes and workers bustling all around us. Amid this development, fragments of the city's imperial past still lingered. The centre of Xi'an was surrounded by a 14th-century wall, and within it a number of Buddhist pagodas stood tall.

Xi'an could have been the end of our journey; it was often considered the easternmost point of the Silk Roads, with much of the silk production happening around here. For our part though, we had chosen to reach Beijing. Marco Polo had reached Xanadu, the first capital of Kublai Khan, some few hundred kilometres northwest of Beijing. Flights to Europe were also much cheaper.

Truth was that we could have ended our journey anywhere. We had never followed Polo's route that closely. Polo had gone through Afghanistan, entering modern China from Kashgar, while we had skipped both entirely.

In our defence, the map of the of the ancient Silk Roads was elusive so we had made one of our own. Polo had been our reference point but he was only one of the many European expeditioners who had travelled along this route. A Roman delegation may have reached China in the 2nd century. Various monks had also embarked on the road with the hope of converting followers. The list of characters was long and colourful.

Less familiar to us were those who had gone in the opposite direction. Books on the history of the Silk Roads often opened either with the story of Alexander the Great headed east, or with that of Zhang Qian's expedition headed west. In the 2nd century before Christ, the diplomat and explorer Zhang Qian was sent by the Han dynasty to explore the valleys of Central Asia. The Chinese army relied on a pony-like breed for its cavalry, but rumours had reached it that somewhere in the Fergana Valley, a taller and stronger breed of horses existed. When Zhang Qian reported he had found these 'heavenly horses', envoys were sent back to take gifts and establish commerce. The envoys were killed and the gifts stolen en route. War followed, the Chinese won and established a puppet state in the region. And with that, China's first trade routes to Central Asia had finally opened.

The more shocking fact about the Silk Roads was that the term was never even used in Polo's texts; it first made it into print in the 19th century – coined by a German geographer by the name of Ferdinand von Richthofen. The term popularised the notion of grand explorers traversing an imaginary highway. However, the Silk Roads were also likely comprised of interconnected but distinct routes. To transport goods and ideas from China to Europe, there was no need for an adventurer to undertake this long journey; a chain of shorter trips could have accomplished the task equally well.

All this I thought to myself, looking at that improvised line we had etched on our map while our pen was now but one line away from ceasing its journey altogether.

Day 102 – Xi'an to Beijing

Again we took a night train, this time to Beijing, this time in first class. We had some spare cash and our days were counted, so we all felt we could afford the luxury of a private room, of sleeping without being observed.

Days 103–104 – Beijing

We entered Beijing in the early morning. From a taxi window we took in the modern cityscape, inebriated with a mix of disbelief and exhaustion. Beijing resembled any other Chinese city we had seen, but with a stronger Western influence – visible in the frequent Starbucks and Irish pub signs.

Our plan was not to sightsee, but to locate a hostel and collapse until lunch. The only endeavour we had planned was for the following day, when we were due to visit the university Anran would join later that summer. The dean of his programme had invited us to a reception, to meet other students and share our story.

The event turned out to be a more elaborate affair than expected. As we stepped foot on the campus, we were welcomed like stars. A small crowd of students waited at the entrance of a building; above them a large banner said 'Welcome to Anran and his team'.

Kaspar and I felt honoured to be part of the team. More than anything, we were all glad to have cleaned up for the occasion, giving ourselves an air of seriousness by each wearing our one shirt. Anran and I had even splurged on new trousers, for ours were in a pitiable state.

The university was a small academy designed to bring foreigners to China. The students were a varied group and it was hard to pin down what they had in common beyond a deep fascination for that country. A few were writing doctorates on niche events in China's history, or studying foreign policy before heading to diplomatic posts. Most were lost souls, still in search of a calling.

The dean was a tall and lively man with a Hawaiian shirt, one that made it clear he was not only American but also living abroad. Speaking to him one could sense there was still a mood of excitement about China, its prospects and its role on the global stage. Only about half a year earlier, Donald Trump had been elected President of the United States with an explicitly anti-China agenda. In this small enclave it was as if that news had not yet arrived, or at least no one had taken it seriously. No one could foretell that Trump's view would be mainstreamed.

The dean showed genuine curiosity for our journey, and drinks were followed by a lavish dinner in one of the university's conference rooms. Around the dinner table we made our first impact with questions like: 'What was your favourite country?' or 'What was the riskiest moment of the journey?' It was a level of attention that we were not used to, and we soon realised that we were not yet ready to tell the story of our journey, nor had we clocked that it had finished the previous day. The dean and the students wanted fun stories; they wanted adventure. What they got were bewildered faces and a hot potato awkwardly jumping around.

As the night progressed, the group thinned and we ended up in the city's famed hutongs. These narrow alleyways, lined with courtyard houses, were oases of peace for the senses. They were mostly dark, with only the soft glow of fairy lights guiding the way. Trees freshened the air, while the distant sound of bicycle bells was faded by the rising murmurs of conversations around bars. On the ground floors, these bars were not much bigger than a room: small bubbles filled with expats.

Here, we were left with a handful of students; the air was jovial, and everyone was pleasantly inebriated. The interrogations became more sporadic, yet one question struck me, a question I would often be asked after the journey. An American student asked, 'Did you find yourself?'

It was a humorous question; but after having told all sorts of stories about our journey it made me wonder whether something tied these together, whether there was an overarching message.

The question itself presumed that it is easier to find oneself by looking far away. As an Italian who had grown up around Europe, I had often asked myself a variant of that question: 'Where will I find myself?' Will it be abroad, or will it be in Italy – after having earned the much-vaunted perspective of the emigrant outsider? If anything, I realised that maybe that horrible phrase of 'being from nowhere' described me after all; I felt at ease everywhere, and yet nowhere – always doubting I understood what it meant to be at ease. It was also hard to escape the accusatory tone in that phrase: one can float endlessly, getting the best from everywhere, leaving nothing behind.

No, I had not found myself. Was there an overarching message to our story? Yes, we had made it to China with the help of others. When on one of our first days I had crashed the car into a tree, a mechanic in Trieste had fixed it without charge. When our car had broken down again in Iran, Shaadi's family had welcomed us into their home. When I had been taken into a military tent for questioning at a football game, two young soldiers had come to find me and take me out. And even when we were not in need, David had invited us for breakfast, Pavel and Yakov had shared their few fish. The sum of those stories was our overarching message. That in the face of foreigners they would never see again, these people had welcomed us like close friends.

I thought of David's phrase as we left his home. His only words in English had been: 'Tell the world about Georgian hospitality, tell the world about us.'

The least we could do was share those stories, to tell those who would listen about David, and the many others like him we had met on our road.

Day 105 – Beijing

The night dragged on as we wandered from one bar to the next. When dawn came, my flight back to Europe was but a few hours away so I returned to the hostel to pack. Kaspar and Anran had planned to stay there a few more days, relishing food and sleep.

Arriving was in no way a success, but I realised that too late. I could have done with more time; I had booked my flight back a week earlier in a moment of exhaustion and now it all felt rushed. I joked with the others, saying I had what must have resembled the baby blues experienced by a new mother. I had accomplished something important to me, leaving nothing to look forward to on the same scale. I felt aimless, with only the past to turn to.

Before leaving Florence, my dad had gifted me a collection of poems by the Greek author Constantine Cavafy. In his poem *Ithaka*, a narrator addresses the reader, talking about an imaginary journey inspired by Homer's epic. The narrator opens the poem with a wish, telling the reader that: 'As you set out for Ithaka / hope your road is a long one / full of adventure, full of discovery'.

Odysseus took ten years to reach his island of Ithaka. Along the way, Laestrygonians, Cyclops and Poseidon all attempted to make his journey harder, to kill him. And yet the reader is told that as long as one has a 'rare excitement' stirring the spirit, there is no reason to fear these evils. Ithaka should be far and difficult to reach.

Cavafy's journey is a metaphor for life, the poem a call to focus on the experience not the destination. A simple message, so beautifully set in Homer's story that I could feel it resonate both literally and metaphorically. Ithaka itself may be a disappointment, the narrator explains, but 'Ithaka gave you the marvelous journey. / Without her you wouldn't have set out. / She has nothing left to give you now'.

My Ithaka had been first Beijing and then home. The first had felt distant, so much so that I had not always been sure I would reach it. Until now, when suddenly it was in sight and the journey felt irreversible.

I could not wander endlessly; this dosage of nomadism had long surpassed my tolerance. But now that I had arrived, I had to find an Ithaka that was further away, or an archipelago of islands, each distant enough from the other, and yet in sight.

As I return to my diary, I realise how memories have a way of being distilled by time. Nostalgia fades on some edges and strengthens on others. I look at my yellowed notes and find myself swaying between moments where I cringe at my younger self and others where I admire a lost courage.

What comes out in writing is an odd mix of two halves. Of the first half, in the last hours of this journey, still mesmerised by memories. And the latter half, writing from a chair – a task regrettably far from adventure.

At 6am my taxi appeared. Kaspar and Anran came outside to say goodbye and we all hugged, suddenly teary-eyed. All three of us were aware of the friendship we now carried. A friendship built on a repertoire of shared stories, one that in the space of a few months had surpassed anything we had done together in the years prior.

We refrained from speaking much, from making promises; no one really knew what to say. Deep down, we understood that a piece of our friendship would stay frozen in that moment. We could have said: 'Until next time, until the next adventure.' But we had never talked about plans. For a short moment in our life, we had been ever-present. We had learned to live treading lightly, not thinking about much outside of the road. And for that final instant, we all yearned to keep it that way.